SPEECHES AND TOASTS

SPEECHES AND TOASTS
FOR ALL OCCASIONS

HOW TO PREPARE THEM
HOW TO DELIVER THEM
with
NUMEROUS MODEL SPEECHES

LONDON
W. FOULSHAM & CO. LTD
NEW YORK   TORONTO   CAPE TOWN   SYDNEY

W. Foulsham & Co. Ltd.
Yeovil Road, Slough, Bucks, England.

ISBN 0-572-00003-0

Made and printed in Great Britain by Compton Printing Ltd.
London and Aylesbury

CONTENTS

CONTENTS

CHAPTER V

CHAPTER VI

CHAPTER VII

CHAPTER VIII

CHAPTER IX

CHAPTER X

CHAPTER XI

CHAPTER XII

CHAPTER XIII

CHAPTER XIV

HOW TO USE THIS BOOK

ORATORY is a gift, but the ability to make a competent speech in public can be readily acquired. This book does not pretend to teach its readers to become brilliant orators. It is a practical and comprehensive guide to speaking, and its object is to help the inexperienced to make a good, competent speech on any occasion.

Whatever kind of speech you have to make, first read Chapter I. Next look through the list of contents to see if a specimen of your speech is included. If it is not, you will probably find one that comes close to it, for the specimens have been carefully chosen to cover a wide field.

Having found your speech, or one closely allied to it, turn to the page indicated and read firstly the hints at the beginning, if there are any, and then the specimen. Finally, run your eye down the list of useful quotations below the specimen. Then go back to Chapter I, and carry out the instructions for preparing the speech that you will deliver.

You could, of course, use the specimen exactly as it stands, but this course is not recommended. It should be used rather as the basis for a speech of your own composition. There are several reasons for this. One is that you will probably want to make a slightly longer speech than most of the specimens. Another is that you will probably want to include a few personal details, and perhaps a humorous story. A third—and the most important—reason is that the speech you make should be phrased in a style similar to that of your ordinary conversation.

If you have got to make a speech on a special subject that is not included among the specimens, follow Chapter I by reading Chapter II. This contains detailed advice on the preparation of a longer speech, and this advice has been given in such a form that it can be adapted to almost any kind of speech that you are required to make.

Although it contains information likely to be of general use to every speaker, Chapter II is intended mainly for those who are required to make specialized speeches on subjects not covered in the specimens in this book. If your speech is covered (or if you can find a specimen on a closely related subject) you do not need to study Chapter II.

After you have prepared your speech on the lines suggested in Chapter I and a specimen, or in Chapters I and II, go on to Chapter III for instructions on delivery. These apply equally to all speeches and toasts.

If you have been called upon to take the chair at a meeting or function, turn to Chapter IV.

A selection of additional quotations of a general nature is given at the end of the book. Both these and the "Useful Quotations" given under the various specimens should be used with care. Some of them are meant to be used only to be contradicted. General advice on the use of quotations is included in Chapter I.

SPEECHES & TOASTS

CHAPTER I

PREPARING A SPEECH: GENERAL ADVICE

SPEECHES are meant to be heard, not read. This may seem obvious, but a good speech cannot be prepared unless it is constantly kept in mind.

You may hear a public speech that impresses you very much. Then you may read the same speech in a newspaper, and wonder why you were so impressed. The speech that sounded so brilliant may seem quite mediocre in print. Perhaps you will conclude that it was the manner of the delivery and the personality of the speaker that made it sound so much better than it reads; but this is rarely the complete explanation. The fact is that it was prepared to be heard, not read—that it was designed to catch the ear, not the eye.

If you reverse the process, and try to prepare a speech by writing an article, and then saying this aloud to an audience, you will not have much success as a speaker. It may be a very good article, but it will not be a good speech. What is more, you yourself will realize this even when you are uttering it.

In certain respects, however, good speeches and good articles have points in common. Both should be clear, not muddled; the arrangements of facts and arguments should be orderly and logical; there should be no waste of words or digressions; and the style should be simple and direct.

FIRST STEPS

Chapter II of this book will give detailed instructions on preparing a speech of some length and importance on a special subject. This first chapter is concerned with all speeches and toasts, and the hints will be general.

The first thing to bear in mind is that whatever the

nature of the speech or toast, it needs preparation in advance. Some persons can get up and make an extempore speech without any preparation; but those who do this well are usually persons who have had experience of public speaking. If you know in advance that you are going to be called on to make a speech, do not leave it till the last minute. Do not imagine that you will be able to "rise to the occasion" without having given it any thought beforehand. Probably you will not.

First of all, then, think of your subject, and decide on what you want to say. Get this firmly into your mind—and then get it down on a piece of paper. You will probably have several ideas, so write them all down. Then get them into order, so that one follows on to another. Cut out repetition and irrelevance. If your speech includes facts, check up to make sure you have got them right.

Eventually you should be able to boil your ideas down to the form of short notes. From these you can write out a model speech. Keep your notes; guidance on how to use these and the model speech will be given in Chapter III. The speech will, of course, need revising several times. It should be written quickly, and it will help considerably if you say it aloud as you write it down. For, as was said at the beginning of this chapter, a speech is not an article. It is meant to be heard, not read; and the surest guide is that if it *sounds* right it is right. Never mind what it *looks* like. Continue to say the words aloud when you revise the speech. You will be surprised to find how different they seem when they are heard instead of read.

YOURSELF AND YOUR AUDIENCE

In preparing the speech you must consider both yourself and your audience. In considering yourself, remember that you have got to deliver the speech. You know your own ability of expression, and you know your limitations. Make concessions to them. Do not set yourself a task that is too hard for you. It is no good composing a beautiful speech if it is too beautiful for you to deliver properly.

Consideration of your audience calls for a good deal of thought. Obviously there will be a considerable difference in style between a speech made at a regimental dinner and an address at a Women's Institute. That is an exaggerated example, and in any case it is hardly likely that your subject would be the same on both occasions. Naturally the subject determines the style to a certain extent, but you must still consider what sort of persons there will be in your audience. Consider their age, their sex, their social status, and especially their relationship to yourself. If you know most of them by their Christian names, don't speak to them as if they were all strangers. If you don't know any of them, don't pretend that you do, even by implication.

Be sincere. Do not prepare to say something that you disbelieve, because it will not ring true, and it is a kind of insult to your audience. Omit anything that might give them offence, but do not say something just to please them unless you can say it with honesty and sincerity.

BREVITY AND SIMPLICITY

Be brief. You rarely hear complaints about a speech being too short, but you hear many people complain that a speech was too long. If you are given a time limit, keep to it; if you are not given a time limit, set one for yourself—and keep to that. And remember that when you time yourself you must make liberal allowance for pauses and—it is to be hoped—for applause and laughter. It is better to finish before your time is up than to go beyond the limit.

Always write your speech in short sentences. They are easier to remember, easier to deliver, and easier for your listeners to grasp. There is nothing so pathetic as hearing a speaker start a sentence and then lose the thread of it, so that he does not know how to bring it to a finish. It is a good plan for beginners especially to use only simple sentences, each consisting of subject, verb, and predicate. Keep away from involved dependent clauses. Writing in short, staccato sentences may not be good style from a literary point of view—although it is better than writing over-involved sentences—but it is the safest form of preparation for a speech. If you normally write in rather long sentences, split them up ruthlessly in the course of revision. Remember that you have got to say them—and breathe! Any faults of this kind that you make in the preparation will come back on you when you have to deliver the speech.

Do not use long words if you know shorter ones that mean

the same thing. Do not say "commence" instead of "begin", or "request" instead of "ask", or "veracious" instead of "true". The use of long words instead of short ones is not a sign of education and scholarship; it is a sign of ignorance. This is such a common fault that it is a good idea to devote one extra revision merely to the purpose of weeding out all words that can be replaced by shorter ones. The use of unnecessarily long words is a bad fault of style even in written English; in a speech it is inexcusable.

Similarly, do not seek uncommon words when you can say the same thing in words that are more familiar. It will only make your speech sound pompous and affected. Those of your audience who do not understand the words will be irritated, and those who do understand them will think you are pretentious.

The best plan is to use only words that you normally use in everyday conversation. If you are trying to use words that are not in your everyday vocabulary, you run the risk of using them incorrectly; and if you do this your audience will laugh at you. Of course it is an advantage for a speaker to have a large vocabulary—but he should not keep one vocabulary for speeches and the other for day-to-day use.

The reason for all this is that you must try, above everything else, to be natural. Be yourself. If you don't the audience will soon spot your pose. Speak as you do in everyday conversation. Do not think that because you are making a speech, you should use more "refined" or "educated" language. If you do, you merely show your lack of refinement and education.

ARCHAISMS AND CLICHES

The use of archaic and obsolete words is an affectation. The reason that words became archaic is that there is no longer any need for them. Usually they have been pushed out of the language by newcomers. So you can never excuse yourself on the grounds that there is no other word to express your meaning. There always is.

Typical archaisms are "methinks", "yclept", "peradventure", "whilom", "behest", "perchance", "certes", "anent", and "damsel".

Equally important, and more difficult to observe, is the necessity to avoid clichés. A cliché is usually an indirect way of expressing a simple idea, which was probably striking when it was first thought of, but which has since been used too frequently and in the wrong context, so that it has become banal and hackneyed and often meaningless. The strongest objection to a cliché is simply that it is hackneyed.

The difficulty arises from the fact that clichés, like catch-phrases, are difficult to avoid. We read them every day in the newspaper, we hear them on the radio, and they are constantly used in normal conversation. Here you may argue that if a speech is to resemble conversation, then clichés ought to be permissible. The answer to this is that clichés are faults in all English, written and spoken, including conversation; and that they are especially irritating when delivered in a public speech.

If you write out the first draft of your speech quickly—and you should do it quickly—then it will almost certainly contain several clichés. Never mind about them while you are writing, but go through the draft afterwards and weed them out.

Here are some typical clichés that should be avoided at all times: "The supreme sacrifice"; "the order of the day"; "a minus quantity"; "conspicuous by his absence"; "the devouring element" (i.e. fire); "slowly but surely"; "not wisely but too well"; "kindly but firmly"; "cruel to be kind"; "a consummation devoutly to be wished"; "the cups that cheer but not inebriate"; "sleep the sleep of the just"; "what would be laughable if it were not tragic"; "has the defects of his qualities"; "take in each other's washing"; "the irony of fate"; "the psychological moment"; "leave severely alone"; "more in sorrow than in anger"; and "the curate's egg".

All these and many other similar expressions were neat or shrewd or witty when they were first used. They were pleasing because of their novelty. Now the novelty has worn off, and they are merely tedious. If you yourself can think of an effective and original way of expressing something, then use it. Then, perhaps, one day you will find it in a list of clichés.

THE USE OF SLANG

The use of slang depends to a great extent on the nature of your audience. It can be used with great effect, but it should always be used with restraint. It is, of course, entirely permissible in the relation of a humorous anecdote where it is called for. Similarly, on special subjects such as sport, slang is almost a technical vocabulary, and is bound to be used. But do not use it for the sake of it; that is a sort of inverted snobbishness, and just as much an affectation as the use of unnecessarily long or unfamiliar words. When in doubt, avoid slang.

Vulgarity should always be avoided. It may get a few cheap laughs, but it will not win over an audience. Avoid even the milder swear-words like "damned". You do not gain anything by using them, and you might cause offence. Similarly avoid blasphemy.

THE USE OF QUOTATIONS

Be careful about using quotations. An apt quotation can be very effective but it must be apt; and do not quote too much. The "useful quotations" given after the specimen speeches and at the end of this book are for guidance only, and should be used only if they really fit into what you are going to say. Never drag in a quotation just to show off your learning. And always avoid Latin and other foreign quotations. A deliberate show of education is the mark of an uneducated person.

You will note that few of the quotations given in this book are very familiar ones. They have been chosen carefully with this in view. A hackneyed quotation is as bad as a cliché—indeed, many clichés are simply hackneyed quotations. Avoid quotations such as "to be or not to be", "more honoured in the breach than in the observance", "the light fantastic toe", "the soft impeachment", etc.

Whenever you do use a quotation, make sure that you quote correctly. Do not say "a little knowledge is a dangerous thing" in error for "A little learning is a dangerous thing", or "Fresh fields and pastures new" in error for "Fresh woods and pastures new". Check your quotations before you use them.

HUMOUR

Some humour is desirable in most speeches and especially toasts, and in many it is absolutely necessary. There are several points to watch here. The first is that you must be sure that your jokes are in good taste. If you are only a little doubtful that they might give offence, even to only a few members of your audience, leave them out. The safest joke is a joke against yourself. The next point is that your humour must be amusing. An original joke is best, because then you can be sure that your audience will not have heard it before. Never repeat a joke you have heard on the radio, for that is bound to be well known. Keep clear of puns; they are not clever. Finally, your jokes must have some bearing on the subject of your speech. If a joke has been obviously "dragged in", it loses its point.

Humorous stories are valuable additions to most speeches, but they must observe the rules stated above. One big advantage about a humorous story is that it is easy to tell. It does not call for great oratory, and you are likely to find it easier to be natural when telling a tale than when speaking more formally. But, again, it must be in good taste; it must be new to the audience; and it must have sufficient bearing on your speech to justify its inclusion.

PROPOSING A TOAST

As will be seen from the specimens in this book, most speeches made on social occasions are in the form of toasts or replies to toasts. All the hints given in this chapter apply equally to toasts as to other speeches, but a few special factors need to be considered.

One is that the proposer of a toast has the advantage of not having to worry about how to end his speech. He simply invites the audience to drink with him, and his closing words are invariably the subject of his toast. This saves a lot of thought, for the ending of a speech is one of the two most difficult parts of it. The other difficult part, of course, is the beginning; and for this, in any social speech and especially in a toast, there is rarely anything better than a humorous reference or a humorous anecdote. It saves the speaker from the danger of being banal; it enables him to capture the interest and good humour of the audience at once; and, because it is easy to relate, it gives him confidence in his ability to make the speech.

One more point must be considered in connection with

toasts. You have been advised to be sincere in your speeches, and not to say anything that you do not believe yourself. This holds good for toasts, too, although they always call for praise of the person or persons whose health is proposed. If you do not feel you can sincerely utter such praise, then try, as tactfully as possible, to decline to propose the toast. If you agree to toast a person whom you can praise with a clear conscience, but of whom you are also critical, you must, for the sake of courtesy, keep your criticism to yourself; but do not exaggerate the praise to make up for it! Exaggerated flattery is bound to be insincere, and audiences are quick to detect insincerity. Never put into your speech anything that you cannot honestly say with conviction.

LAST-MINUTE ALTERATIONS TO A SPEECH

When you prepare your speech you should always frame it in such a way that you can change it or add to it at the last minute—if necessary, in the course of the function at which it is to be made.

This is very important. For one thing, you may be anticipated by a previous speaker saying something—perhaps telling a story—that is already down in your speech. You cannot say the same thing after him, so you must remove it from your speech and, to preserve continuity if not length, close the gap. Another possible reason for having to make a last-minute alteration occurs when a previous speaker has said something to which you will be expected to refer or reply. You should not ignore this even if you can do so without making it obvious. Audiences are always favourably impressed when they hear something that the speaker could not possibly have thought out in advance.

A reply to a toast, of course, almost always involves last-minute changes and additions. However, such a speech should still be prepared in advance in the normal way, the only difference being that it should be made as general as possible. Usually you can anticipate the sort of things that will be said by the proposer of the toast, and your draft reply should answer these. But, of course, you must be ready to change your reply if the things you expect are not said; and you must be equally ready to answer points made by the proposer that you have not anticipated. In this sense replying to a toast is extempore speaking; but that does not mean that the main part of the speech cannot be prepared in advance.

When you have to make an addition of this sort to your prepared speech, the best plan is to make it at the beginning. Usually this is the most suitable place for it. The audience will still have the point fresh in mind, and will be expecting you to reply—and, moreover, will be delighted if you reply quickly, apparently without having had much time to think. But the main advantage to you is that you can deal with the addition at once, and can then get on with your prepared speech without having to worry about it any more.

GOOD GRAMMAR

Your speech should, of course, be grammatical. There are no special rules about grammar for speeches; in this respect the spoken word does not differ from the written word. You should speak as grammatically as you write, and if you fail on grammar this has nothing to do with speech-making.

Still, a few points may be emphasized. The first is that being grammatical does not mean being pedantic. Remember that grammar was made for man, not man for grammar. Grammar is a good servant, but a bad master. Good style, in writing as in speaking, is certainly grammatical; but excessive or misplaced regard for grammatical rules may ruin style altogether.

At school you were probably taught that you should never end a sentence with a preposition. It is a sound rule, but sometimes it has to be broken. The alternative is to produce an ugly and ungainly sentence. This is bad in writing, and worse in speaking. Winston Churchill once ridiculed it brilliantly. He had to read a report prepared by a Civil Servant, who had learnt the rule too thoroughly, and performed all sorts of verbal gymnastics to prevent prepositions from getting to the ends of his sentences. When he had finished reading the report Churchill wrote in the margin: "This is the sort of English up with which I cannot put."

Probably the best books on grammar ever written are H. W. Fowler's *Modern English Usage* and *The King's English*, both published by the Oxford University Press. Both are entertaining reading as well as soundly instructive.

Fowler had the highest standards, but was broad-minded and tolerant to a degree unique for a grammarian. He pointed out, for example, that more bad English is written by those who try to avoid splitting infinitives (and yet do not really understand what a split infinitive is) than those who split infinitives carelessly and cheerfully. You often see a needlessly ugly phrase such as "really to be understood", obviously phrased in this ungainly fashion because the writer had the mistaken belief that "to be really understood" contained a split infinitive. Fowler did not recommend splitting infinitives by any means; but he regarded the practice as a lesser evil than distorting sentences to escape from imaginary split infinitives. This is another example of the dangers of trying to be "too grammatical".

FINAL HINTS

When you prepare your speech always bear in mind that your primary object is to make your meaning clear, and the words you use must be chosen primarily for this purpose. The clearest way of saying a thing is usually the simplest. Avoid unnecessarily long words and circumlocutions. Do not say "I obtained not a little assistance from the arm of the law" when you mean "I got a lot of help from the constable", or "we came to the parting of the ways" when you mean "we parted".

Never use two words when one will do. Always try for the maximum economy of language. Do not keep saying words like "very" and "quite". Wasting words takes up your time, obscures your meaning, and irritates your audience.

Chapter II

PREPARING A SPEECH: INSTRUCTIONS IN DETAIL

THE last chapter contained general instructions on preparing speeches and toasts for all occasions; and if you are required only to make a brief speech at a social gathering or to propose a toast, you will not need to go any further into the matter of preparation. If, however, you are required to make a longer and more important speech on a particular subject—for example, at a public meeting, or a meeting of a literary or similarly serious society, or as a principal in an organized debate—then more careful preparation will be necessary. It is for the preparation of a speech of the latter kind that this chapter has been written.

It was said in the last chapter that a speech is not an article, and that preparing something to be heard is a very different matter from preparing something to be read. This applies to every kind of speech, and it must be borne in mind throughout the preparations. You must never forget that your medium is to be the spoken and not the written word.

The secret of preparing a good speech on a definite subject is in method. However good your ideas are, unless you follow a method you will not be able to compose a coherent and effective speech. The same method can be used for all speeches, and once it has been mastered, the work of preparation becomes quite straightforward.

To make the method clearer here, it will be applied to a practical example. Let us suppose that you have to deliver a speech on "The Need for Prison Reform". (If you think that prisons do not need reform, do not let that influence your study of this chapter. This subject has been chosen as an example because it is fairly typical of the sort of speech commonly delivered at public meetings, literary and debating societies, etc.)

Now presumably you will already have some ideas on the subject, otherwise you would not have been asked, or you would not have agreed, to make the speech. So before you do anything else, jot your ideas down on a piece of paper.

Let them come naturally—do not try to "invent" any. There is no need to try to get them in any sort of order at this stage, but it is a good plan to put them under two headings —"Facts" and "Arguments".

Regarding the "Arguments", you will see that this speech is of a partisan nature. It is to be one-sided. All speeches in debates, and most speeches at public and club meetings, are one-sided. Only the chairman, who makes a brief summing up, is expected to be impartial. Your subject here is "The *Need* for Prison Reform", and you are expected to make a case. If the occasion for the speech is a debate, the opposite point of view will also be expressed. You must bear this in mind, and try to anticipate and disarm criticisms, and be careful not to say anything that will give your opponents an opportunity to gain debating points.

As you make your first notes, then, let your thoughts run freely, and you will find that one idea leads to another. Do not reject any idea because it does not seem to fit; selection will come later. Do not worry about how you are going to express your ideas, or the right words to use. Simply put everything down as it occurs to you, and go on in this way until you have run dry. Then put the piece of paper away and leave it for a day or so.

Now go back to your notes, and sort them out. This means simply grouping the ideas together. You should not try to put the groups into a definite order. Simply link up ideas that are of a similar nature. During this process you will find that fresh ideas will probably occur to you, so put these down as well. As before, do not try to "force" ideas if they are not already there.

Now make a note of the facts that need to be looked up or checked. For this purpose you will need encyclopædias and other reference books, most of which you will probably be able to find in the local library. The wisest plan is to check every fact you can. In a debate, especially, it is vital that you should not make any error of fact, even of detail. An otherwise excellent speech can be utterly ruined by a factual mistake. If you are in doubt about a fact, and cannot check it properly, leave it out.

Next test the validity of your arguments. Ask yourself if they are really convincing. If they do not convince you, it is unlikely that they will convince your audience. If your speech includes only one unconvincing argument, the audience will be more sceptical about your sound arguments.

Now consider whether your knowledge of the subject is really adequate. On a subject like prison reform you will help yourself a great deal if you can obtain permission to visit a prison. Then you will be able to speak with first-hand authority; and, of course, the visit itself will certainly give you fresh ideas. On this subject, too, you ought to read up reports of Royal Commissions and similar documents. There is a large literature on the subject, and you ought to read as many books as you can. But you must not copy from the books of others. It is your speech, and it will not be a good one unless it expresses your ideas. That is why you have been advised to write down your own ideas before delving into the literature on the subject.

A large part of your reading should be of books by opponents of prison reform. Study their arguments, and try to find answers to them. If you are speaking in a debate, you may be sure that opposing arguments that have already been published will be repeated by your opponents. Be ready for them. Anticipate them, and "kill" them before they are uttered.

It will be a good idea to seek information about books and other sources of material from a society that is devoted to the subject on which you are to speak. Thus for prison reform you could approach the Howard League of Penal Reform. You will find the address of this and other similar societies in *Whitaker's Almanack*. But do not do this until you have first put down your own ideas.

In the course of these researches you will doubtless add to your list of facts and modify some of your arguments. It is a good idea to make these additions and alterations in red ink, so that you will later be able to see which of your notes represent original ideas. These original ideas should remain the basis of your speech.

When you have got all your material—that is, ideas from your brain and facts from reference sources—the time has come for you to compose the framework of your speech.

Generally speaking, it may be said that a speech consists of three parts: the beginning, or pre-oration; the middle, or discussion; and the end, or peroration.

The importance of the pre-oration is that it should capture the attention of the audience. Avoid saying anything banal or obvious. For example, "The prisons in this country are in grave need of reform" would be a weak opening sentence.

On a social occasion, or when the speech is of a lighter character, it is a good idea to begin with a touch of humour. If, for example, you were speaking in a debate on whether men were better cooks than women, you could start with a personal domestic anecdote. In a speech on a subject like prison reform, however, a humorous opening would be out of place, so you must think of a different sort of introduction.

A topical reference is often a good solution of this problem. Look through the newspapers, and pick out a Court case that has aroused general public interest. Let us suppose that a burglar named John Smith, aged twenty-one, has been sent to prison for three years. Now take a fresh piece of paper, and write down:

(1) John Smith, burglar, 21. 3 years.

Now your subject is prisons, and you have got to get on to this theme at once. The case of John Smith makes it easy. You have brought home to your audience the reality of crime, and now you are going to bring home to them the reality of prisons. You do this by asking them if they have any idea of where, and to what, John Smith is going; what is in store for him during the next three years?

So you write down, still under the same heading (1):

Where is he going?

Now you enlarge on this from your original list of notes. This is where a personal visit to a prison will be of great help to you. Failing that, you must take facts obtained from reference books, reports of Royal Commissions, etc. This part of the speech should be brief, but it must be vivid. Do not exaggerate. Do not even express any opinion yet. In this part of the speech you need only facts.

So enlarge your heading (1) with the note:

Personal visit (or report of Royal Commission, etc.).

That concludes the preparation of the introduction to your speech. Now you come to the middle; and this can be divided roughly into four parts, which may be summarized under the following headings:

(2) Statement of the proposition or "argument" that you wish to prove.

(3) The evidence in detail.
(4) The summary of evidence.
(5) Exposition of the conclusion logically to be drawn from such evidence.

These headings will, of course, want sub-divisions. The evidence in detail, will occupy a large part of your speech, and will need to be split up into several parts.

Now let us take heading (2)—the statement of your proposition or "argument". You want to prove something—in this case, that prisons need reform. (That is implicit in the title of your speech.) Therefore you must say first of all why they need reform. You must say what, in your opinion, is wrong with them.

You will find your material in your original notes, under the heading "Arguments". Select them carefully, leaving out anything that seems weaker or less relevant to the question. Arrange them in order, and then make notes of the salient points.

Let us suppose for the sake of the illustration that you consider that the main thing wrong with the prisons is that they are out of date. Society's attitude to criminals has changed, but parallel changes in prison buildings and, to some extent, the whole system, have lagged behind. Most of them were built in the days when it was generally accepted that the punishment should fit the crime; now society considers generally that the punishment should fit the criminal. The prisons were built before the idea of reformation and rehabilitation of prisoners was accepted; and prison administration, while greatly improved, is still in need of reform.

Under the heading (2), then, you will write down:

(2) Prisons need reform.
   Punishment fit the criminal, not the crime.
   Buildings no longer suitable.
   Administration needs modernization.

So you move on to the next heading—the evidence in detail. Its quantity will be governed by the amount of time you are allowed for your speech. Certainly you will have to select ruthlessly, and even the facts that are included will have to be compressed. Naturally you will want to get as many facts in as you can; but do not try to include everything if this means that you will not be able to do anything justice.

It is better to leave out the less impressive facts and make the most of the strongest ones. And do not hesitate to weed out anything that is not strictly relevant or that does not fit in with its neighbours. There must be no suspicion of digression in your speech. It must be arranged in a logical and orderly manner, with each point leading naturally on to the next.

The evidence, of course, comes from your original notes under the heading "Facts". Take what you need, and arrange it in the most suitable order. Then write down your notes. They may be something like this:

(3) Physical overcrowding.
   Poor hygiene and sanitation.
   More "open prisons" needed.
   Stultifying influence of unnecessary petty restrictions.
   Inadequate provision of useful employment.
   Lack of proper educational facilities.
   Insufficient classification and segregation of prisoners.
   Insufficient constructive reformatory work.

Your next heading is the summary of evidence, and this will be much briefer. For example:

(4) Overcrowding and bad conditions.
   Repressive influences.
   Insufficient rehabilitation.

Now you come to the logical conclusion to be drawn from all the foregoing. This is the most important part of your speech, and it must be clear and forceful. It must also anticipate possible criticisms of your argument and, if possible, disarm them. One obvious such criticism is finance; and you might answer this in advance by pointing out that unless conditions are changed there will be more "chronic" criminals, and that crime costs the nation more than the reforms would do—that is that, far from not being able to afford to make reforms, we cannot afford not to make them.

Also you must bring out the most constructive features of your argument. In this particular example, of course, there is constructive criticism from the beginning of the speech; but in general the way to present an argument is to criticize the present state of affairs first, pointing out the things that are wrong, and then say how they could be made better.

Bearing these points in mind, you may summarize your logical conclusions as follows:

> (5) System out of date.
> Theory not put into practice.
> Need for new buildings and better administration.
> Cannot afford *not* to reform prisons.

Finally comes your peroration, and this is perhaps the most difficult part of your speech. Like the pre-oration, it should be striking, but in a different way: your object is to leave something in your listeners' ears—something that they will continue to remember after you have sat down. A really apt quotation makes a good peroration; failing that, try to end with a trenchant epigram or a paradox.

In this case a possible theme for the peroration is a denial of sentimentality. Prison reformers are often labelled by their opponents as well-meaning but unrealistic persons, who do not understand the harsh facts of crime. You can anticipate this criticism and at the same time startle your listeners by declaring bluntly that you have no time for sentiment in this matter, and demand that they look at it from a strictly practical point of view. Returning indirectly to the financial angle, ask them if we can afford to allow crime to continue at its present high level. Say bluntly that there are only two ways of preventing criminals from returning to crime: one is to execute them, or at least keep them in prison until they die; the other is to reform them. At present a fatal middle course is being pursued. Modern society would not allow the extermination of all criminals, and therefore the only sane course is to try to reform them.

Put the notes for the peroration as follows:

> (6) No time for sentiment.
> Exterminate or reform.

Now you have the whole pattern of your speech. Your notes will read as follows:

(1) *Pre-oration or introduction*

> John Smith, burglar, 21. 3 years.
> Where is he going?
> Personal visit (or report of Royal Commission, etc.).

(2) *Proposition or "argument"*

> Prisons need reform.
> Punishment fit the criminal, not the crime.
> Buildings no longer suitable.
> Administration needs modernization.

(3) *Evidence in detail*

> Physical overcrowding.
> Poor hygiene and sanitation.
> More "open prisons" needed.
> Stultifying influence of unnecessary petty restrictions.
> Inadequate provision of useful employment.
> Lack of proper educational facilities.
> Insufficient classification and segregation of prisoners.
> Insufficient constructive reformatory work.

(4) *Summary of evidence*

> Overcrowding and bad conditions.
> Repressive influences.
> Insufficient rehabilitation.

(5) *Logical conclusions*

> System out of date.
> Theory not yet put into practice.
> Need for new buildings and better administration.
> Cannot afford not to reform prisons.

(6) *Peroration, or conclusion*

> No time for sentiment.
> Exterminate or reform.

Now before you go any further, try to reduce these notes to a more compact form. Put them into a kind of private shorthand, to which you alone hold the key, trying to compress ideas into single words which will be sufficient to remind you of the longer notes. For example:

(1) John Smith, 21, 3 years. Where going? Visit.
(2) Reform. Punishment fit criminal. Buildings unsuitable. Administration.
(3) Overcrowding. Hygiene. "Open prisons." Restrictions. Employment. Education. Classification. Constructive work.

(4) Overcrowding. Repression. Rehabilitation.
(5) Out of date. Theory—practice. Buildings, administration. Cannot afford.
(6) Sentiment. Exterminate or reform.

The purpose of this abridged set of notes will be explained in the next chapter.

Now return to the longer notes, numbered (1) to (6). This is the framework of your speech, so before you go any further, read the notes again as critically as you can, and ask yourself (a) if they include anything that does not fit in or that could be omitted without weakening the argument; (b) if there is any repetition or bad arrangement that is likely to cause the speech to be longer than it need be; (c) if the existing arrangement is logical and orderly, so that each idea naturally leads to the next; and (d) if this arrangement of your ideas really represents what you want to say.

Next turn to your original notes, and read through the facts and arguments that were not selected for inclusion. If any of these seems too important to be left out, consult the framework again to see if you can modify it to include the omitted matter.

The next step is to write out your speech. Do this quickly, without bothering to spend minutes on trying to find the best words. Speak it aloud as you write it, but do not try to revise as you go along. Do not ramble away from your headings. If you get new ideas, put them down on a separate piece of paper, for consideration after the rough draft is finished.

When your speech is finished, read it through aloud, once. Then settle down to revise it. You cannot spend too much time on this. You should polish it, rephrase it, and constantly try to improve it in every possible way. Be highly critical of it. If a word does not seem quite right, try to find a better one. You will find synonyms in any dictionary, and many more in Roget's *Thesaurus*. Consider each argument, and see if you can find a clearer and more forceful way of expressing your points.

When at last your revision is complete, put the speech away for a day or so. Then get it out and again read it aloud, and make any further revisions that seem necessary. There will be some!

Now time the speech, allowing for pauses. If it is too long, cut it ruthlessly. Do not keep telling yourself that if you cut it down you will not do justice to your subject. Remember that you will have left your strongest arguments to the end, and they are not going to have much effect if half your audience has gone to sleep before they are delivered.

When you have got your speech down to the allotted length—a little less is better than a little more—polish it again. You can go on polishing at intervals right up until the time has come for you to make the speech, and after each revision it will look more and more like a finished article.

Finally, take out your set of abridged notes and compare them with the speech. Modify them to take into account the revisions you have made. This check will serve the additional purpose of showing whether you have kept to the logical and orderly arrangement of your ideas.

The next step is to prepare for the delivery, and this will be described in the following chapter.

CHAPTER III

DELIVERING A SPEECH

IT has been said that the best advice on making a speech is embodied in the simple injunction to "stand up, speak up, and shut up". The question of shutting up has already been dealt with in the remarks (in Chapter I) on the necessity for brevity. This chapter will deal with the equally important matters of standing up and speaking up.

Before the actual delivery is discussed, however, a few words must be said about the question of memorizing the speech. It has been shown how each speech should be prepared and written out beforehand; and the next thing to decide is how this written speech is to be turned into speech as it is spoken.

MEMORIZING THE SPEECH

There are four ways of memorizing a speech. It can be read; it can be learnt by heart and recited; it can be memorized more broadly, but not delivered word for word; or it can be so memorized that the speaker will, with the aid of a few notes, be able to deliver it nearly in the form in which it was prepared.

Reading a speech is the very worst method, and it should be avoided. It has many disadvantages. The main one, of course, is that it never sounds really convincing, and the audience is unsympathetic from the beginning. There is the famous case of the speaker who stood up, solemnly produced a sheaf of papers from his pocket, adjusted his glasses, and began to read: "It is with considerable surprise that I see so many faces of old friends before me." Of course the old friends laughed—but only because he was reading it, and thus giving away the fact that he had written those words before he knew how many old friends would be there. Another disadvantage of reading a speech is that the speaker does not allow himself the opportunity of modifying his speech in the light of what has been said by previous speakers.

The necessity for this was mentioned in Chapter I.

This latter disadvantage applies equally to learning by heart and then reciting. This is not such a bad method as reading, but it is hardly to be recommended. Unless the speaker is naturally a brilliant actor, the speech will probably sound flat and artificial. There is a further danger. Unlike an actor, the speaker has no prompter, and if, through an attack of nerves, he "loses his place", utter confusion and probably panic will result.

The third method is excellent for the practised speaker, but hardly recommended for the beginner. It involves a heavy strain on the memory, and adroitness in the use of words.

The fourth method is probably the most suitable for all but accomplished speakers. The work of memorizing the speech is done automatically in the preparation, and in the case of a long speech the notes will simply be the "abridged notes" referred to in Chapter II. You may be dismayed at the thought of not repeating every word of the speech that you took so much trouble to prepare, write, and revise; but you can take comfort from the fact that your memory will almost certainly prove an excellent "sieve", retaining the best things and rejecting the worthless.

The author had a lesson in the value of this "sieve" early in his career as a public speaker. By chance he had been asked by two different societies to speak on the same subject within a matter of a few days. Rather unwisely, he prepared exactly the same speech for both occasions, although he knew the audiences were dissimilar in type. His wife (who was present on both occasions) noticed that the two speeches as delivered differed from each other in many particulars. Afterwards he and his wife went over the original draft of the speech, and made an illuminating discovery. The memory had acted as a censor as well as a sieve, having done what the speaker himself ought to have done in preparing the speeches: it had rejected different things on the two occasions, according to their unsuitability for the respective audiences. There is a psychological explanation for this phenomenon which does not concern us here. It is enough to say that there is a censor in the human mind, which often saves a speaker from committing indiscretions that he might regret.

Where this fourth method of memorizing the speech is

used, the notes should be written—or, better, typed—on a postcard. They must be clear enough for you to read merely by glancing down. Unless you are short-sighted, do not hold the card while delivering the speech, but merely place it on the table in front of you. Consult it with the smallest possible ostentation, preferably during enforced pauses for cheers or laughter. A quick glance down should be enough to assure you of the next point in your speech.

Good delivery can come only with practice, and the best practice is to go into a room alone, taking only your card of notes, and address an imaginary audience. Having decided not to learn the speech by heart and then recite it, do not keep breaking off while you search your memory for the exact words you wrote. You must be prepared to sacrifice these, and you need not think that you were wasting your time in taking so much trouble in composing the speech. Had you not written it out in full, and constantly revised it, you would find it much harder to acquire fluency.

That, of course, is another reason why this method is preferable to both reading and learning by heart. However hard you may have tried to bear in mind that you were composing a speech and not writing an article, you will almost certainly have included a few sentences that are expressed more in the manner of the written than the spoken word. Your "memory censor" will come to your help here by rejecting purely "literary" expressions and forcing you to substitute expressions suitable for oratory. This will help greatly to make the speech sound natural.

That you should try to make the speech sound natural is another way of saying that you should try to persuade your audience that it was *not* prepared beforehand! To this extent the aim of good delivery is to deceive. Firstly you prepared your speech with great care; now, in delivering it, you use all your ability to make it sound spontaneous. If the speech were read this would be impossible, and if it were learnt by heart and then recited it would be very difficult.

While you are practising your delivery of the speech with the aid of your notes, you will probably find that, in spite of all your careful revision, it still contains some things that sound stilted, and more suitable expressions will occur to you. Adopt them; do not think that just because your speech has been beautifully written out or typed, therefore it should not be touched. It is never too late to improve—and in the matter of speaking, your tongue is always wiser than your pen.

You may find it helpful to try out your speech on a member of your family or a friend. This practice may be useful, but there are dangers in it. You will almost certainly get some criticism, and you must be careful how far you accept it. Consider first if your experimental audience is of the same type as the audience for which your speech has been composed. For example, a maiden aunt is not the best person to give an opinion on a speech made for an Old Boys' Dinner. Then bear in mind that there is a tremendous difference between the effect of a speech on a single listener who knows you intimately and its effect on an audience of two or three hundred who do not know you nearly so well. A humorous reference or a joke may fall flat in rehearsal, and yet be greeted with a lot of laughter when it comes to the delivery before the full audience. Remember that it is always easier to amuse a lot of people together than one individual. Even a feeble joke can cause great amusement if there are enough people hearing it together. That is why radio comedians like to have a studio audience.

"STAGE FRIGHT"

Now we come to the actual delivery—the standing up and speaking up. Your first difficulty, at least in your maiden speech, will probably be in controlling your nerves. You will be afflicted with what actors call "stage fright".

Overcoming stage fright is solely a matter of confidence, and therefore the first lesson you must learn is that it *can* be overcome. It will help you if you realize that it is a universal affliction of speakers, and not peculiar to you. Remember that the most eloquent speakers whom you hear now were probably very nervous and "stage struck" when they first began to speak in public.

There is only one certain way of overcoming nervousness, and that is simply practice. This is the reason why it is such a good idea to join a debating society as a preliminary to public speaking. Failing this, practise by yourself either in an empty room or to the rest of your family—if they will let you! But whenever you practise, do it properly. Make it a dress rehearsal, and try to imagine that you are addressing a real audience; otherwise it will be of little help. Practise with the speech you have prepared, and also with some of the specimens in the book. To begin with you can simply read these aloud; then try to deliver similar speeches without the book.

When the time comes for you to deliver your speech, you will probably find this simple little exercise helpful. Just before you are about to rise, deflate your lungs and then take in a full breath of air and expel it slowly. Do this two or three times. It will increase the supply of oxygen to your blood, and thus steady your nerves.

Finally, be careful of seeking "Dutch courage" at the bar. A drink may bolster up your confidence temporarily and act as a stimulant; but too much alcohol will certainly be disastrous. It will ruin your delivery, and cloud your brain at a time when it should be at its sharpest.

As nerves are felt most at the beginning of a speech, you should have considered this matter in preparing your pre-oration. There is no point in starting with a brilliant sentence if you do not feel you are capable of delivering it properly. A humorous allusion or anecdote it always a good beginning for the novice, because it is the easiest to relate. Automatically you slip into a natural, conversational style, and the battle of nerves is won.

STANDING UP

Every public speaker must know how to stand properly. But before you stand you have got to rise, and the importance of the way you do this is rarely considered. In fact it is very important indeed.

When you are called upon to get up, you probably feel slightly sick, you want to avoid the gaze of the audience and your legs seem flabby. Unless you get a grip on yourself you will probably get up slowly and reluctantly, and begin with your knees still bent, while your feet are shuffling miserably on the floor.

That is no good at all. Get a grip on yourself at once, stand up smartly, and face your audience squarely. If you do this you will find that your nerves are much better than they were a few seconds earlier. There is nothing like a show of confidence to make you feel confident.

Your position in standing should be easy and comfortable. The first rule is simple: Don't pose. Don't try to stand like a soldier on parade. Place your feet apart and put yourself at ease.

Don't loll in a slovenly fashion. Stand upright, and don't begin speaking until you have completed the process of standing up. A momentary pause should be made before the speech is begun. It is better to put the weight of your body on one foot rather than on both. For one thing this is less tiring; for another, it enables you to turn from one side to the other. But that is not to say that you should be constantly swaying when you are speaking. On the contrary, you should keep your body as still as possible. Above all, keep your feet still.

The position of your head is most important. You will notice that at most public meetings the speaker stands on a raised platform, so that he looks slightly down on his audience. The reason for this is that it is easier to speak if the head is tilted forward and downward a little. If it is held too high the muscles of the throat will be restricted.

Your hands will probably worry you at first. They will seem enormous, and you will not know what to do with them. There are several things that you should not do with them. Don't let them hang limply by your sides, or you will feel—and look—ill at ease. Don't fold them across your chest, or you will not be able to breathe properly. Don't try to rest them on the table in front of you, as this will probably be too low, and so you will have to bend forward all the time.

There are four places to put your hands. You can grasp the lapels of your jacket, although this is not recommended; it makes you want to fidget nervously. A better place is the back of a chair or the rail of the platform. This will be of the proper height, and you will find that having something to grasp increases your confidence. A very safe place is behind your back. The fourth possibility is in your pockets, and on an informal occasion this is as good as any. But if you decide to put your hands in your pockets, keep them there; and don't jingle keys or money, or you will irritate your audience.

The position of the hands, like everything else, is a problem that disappears after practice. The experienced speaker does not think about his hands, and they naturally go into a suitable place.

The matter of gesticulation is simple. First of all, never "invent" a gesture. Do not make a deliberate movement of your hands or arms in an attempt to give emphasis to your words. It will make you look like a clown. Therefore, do not think about gestures at all—until they come of their own accord. You will find, as you warm to your subject, that you are making spontaneous gestures. These are natural, so do not attempt to alter them. Let them come. The only time you need interfere is when they are coming too frequently. Remember that the British as a nation do not like a lot of demonstrativeness, and if you find that your hands and arms are moving about too much, you must control them.

Finally, you must consider your eyes. Do not look at the floor. Do not look at the ceiling. Look at the audience—at the back of the audience for preference. If you are speaking from notes, learn to take them in with an occasional quick glance downward, preferably during a pause.

CORRECT BREATHING

Speaking, like singing, requires correct breathing. The first rule is simply that you should throw your chest out. In other words, take as much air into your lungs as you can, and never exhaust them completely. Keeping your shoulders back and your abdomen drawn in slightly will help you to do this. Breathe in more air at every opportunity. Inhale only through the nose if you can; it is important that the taking of a breath should be accomplished in silence. If you are speaking into a microphone this is essential.

Give yourself plenty of opportunity for taking in fresh breaths. Do not attempt to deliver too many words without a pause, or you will find that you are forced to make an unintended pause simply to take in more air. This can spoil the effect of your speech.

SPEAKING UP

It almost goes without saying that a speech should be audible, yet inaudibility is one of the commonest errors in public speaking today. It is also the least excusable, for audibility is quite simple even for those who have not got naturally powerful voices.

Speak clearly, and open your mouth. Don't mumble. Don't fall into the common fault of dropping your voice at the end of sentences. Aim at the back of your audience. There is no need to shout to make your voice carry. Do not speak too rapidly. If you are interrupted by applause or laughter, wait until silence has returned before going on. The same applies to other interruptions. Incidentally, if members of your audience are ill-mannered enough to whisper while you are speaking, do not glare at them; simply pause, and they will soon stop whispering. The same applies if there is a noise of plate and glass.

During practice you will have divided your speech up into phrases, with pauses between them. You will have found from experience that "punctuation" in speaking is not the same as in writing. You have to make many additional pauses when there are no commas. These pauses should be made intelligently, however. A good pause can be more effective than words. Also, pauses should be of different lengths. Generally speaking, the more important the words that *follow* the pause, the longer the pause should be. Take these pauses seriously, because they are a vital part of your speech. Fit your breathing to the pauses, not the pauses to your breathing.

Here is an example of the correct use of pauses. It is the famous tribute made by Winston Churchill to the R.A.F. during the Second World War. The sentence reads:

"Never in the field of human conflict was so much owed by so many to so few."

It will be seen that this sentence does not contain a single comma or other punctuation mark until the full stop at the end. Yet if it were spoken without any pauses it would lose all its effectiveness.

Divide the sentence as follows:

"Never—*very short pause*—in the field of human conflict —*short pause*—was so much—*short pause*—owed by so many —*longer pause*—to so few."

Not all these pauses are necessary for breathing; but they are all needed to give the words the full significance that they deserve. It will be seen that the longest pause (of course it is long only by comparison) comes before the most important words—"to so few".

Closely linked with the subject of pauses is the use of emphasis. Again, there is a big difference between the written and the spoken word. When a writer wants to emphasize a word or phrase, he puts it in *italics*. Good writers use italics very sparingly. In speaking, however, "verbal italics" are necessary on a much bigger scale.

For example, take the simple sentence: "It can be done; it will be done." In writing this, no italics are needed; but if it is spoken, the verbs must be emphasized, so that it becomes: "It *can* be done; it *will* be done." Emphasis, like the pause, should be varied. Do not over-emphasize everything, or your emphasis will lose its value, and you will have nothing left for really important words. Your emphasis should range from light to heavy, and be used with care.

MANNER OF SPEAKING

Your manner of speech will depend upon the occasion and the audience. However, certain general principles apply to all circumstances.

Do not be pompous or patronizing. You must "win over" the audience. Don't talk down. On the other hand, don't try to be over-familiar, or you may appear vulgar.

Vary your tone according to the subject matter of your speech. Avoid monotony of delivery. Modulate your tones. Be sincere. Put all the meaning you can into your words— but don't be theatrical. Whatever else your manner is, it must be natural. It should be a polished version of your normal conversational manner. Even if the members of the audience do not know you, they will be quick to sense artificiality of manner, and the reception of your speech will suffer accordingly.

Do not punctuate your speech with "um's" and "ah's". You may not realize it yourself, but they are very irritating to the audience. Watch for this danger from the very start, for it can become a habit that is increasingly difficult to cure. The chief cause of this fault is, of course, insufficient preparation of the speech. The other main cause is lack of concentration. The speaker says "um" or "ah" to gain time while he thinks of what he is going to say next. If you must pause to think, then let it be a silent pause.

ELOCUTION AND ARTICULATION

It was said earlier in this chapter that you do not need to have a powerful voice to make yourself audible and, in fact, it is not volume that makes it possible for your audience to hear what you are saying. It is, rather, the way you say it.

Speaking is a manner of communication, and correct speaking is nothing more than clear speaking. Much snobbishness has been said and written about the question of accent, and this can be disposed of very briefly. If you have a Scottish or Yorkshire or any other accent, do not try to conceal it. It is nothing to be ashamed of—indeed, it gives character to your delivery. The only thing you have to watch is that it should not prevent your audience from understanding what you are saying.

So use your natural accent. Do not try to adopt, for example, an "Oxford accent" in the mistaken belief that it is more refined. This will be an affectation, and you will neither convince nor please your audience.

Whatever your accent—however you pronounce words— you must make sure that you pronounce them clearly and distinctly. The commonest error in elocution is failure to pronounce certain letters.

Slackness over the letter "h" is well known. Dropping the initial "h" in its commonest form, as in words like "house" (" 'ouse") and "holiday" (" 'oliday"). The reverse of the error is to put an "h' where it does not belong, as in "ambition" ("hambition") and especially words beginning with an "h" mute such as "heir", "honest", and "hour". These twin faults can often be avoided by care over the pronunciation of the definite article ("the"). When this comes before a vowel or "h" mute, it should be pronounced "thee"; when before a consonant, it should be pronounced simply "th" with a short vowel sound to separate it from the first letter of the following word. If this rule is observed it becomes almost physically impossible to go wrong.

A more common fault is ignoring the letter "h" in words like "what", "when", and "where". Yet another common error is to run on words like "is he" into something that sounds like "izzee".

The first rule in elocution is that each word should be pronounced separately, and that all the letters that are meant to be pronounced should be pronounced. This may involve making a brief pause between words, but the gain in clearness and distinctness is immeasurable. Letter that often get lost are final "d's" and "t's" and "k's" and the "g" in words ending in "-ing". To say "that time" or "and did" correctly involves a definite pause between words. In practising this you may find at first that it sounds stilted and awkward; but with further practice you will eventually find it just as easy to pronounce the words correctly as incorrectly.

The pronunciation of the final "r" depends on whether or not a vowel begins the next word. In the expression "weather bulletin", for example, the "r" at the end of "weather" is barely pronounced; but if you say "tar and feathers" you must pronounce the "r" in "tar" distinctly. You must not, of course, put in an "r" to join a word ending with a vowel to a word beginning with a vowel, as in "the idea of" ("the idea*r* of") or "I saw an engine" ("I saw*r* an engine"). This error is just as bad as putting in an "h" where it does not belong.

All these errors can be avoided if you practise saying each word slowly and distinctly, and pronouncing every letter that is not mute. It is a good plan to practise speaking before a looking glass, to make sure that you are using your lips, teeth, and tongue in the proper way. Bad vowel sounds are usually the result of failure to open the mouth properly; slackness over the letters "t" and "d" is caused by failure to bring the tongue in proper relation to the teeth.

Most dictionaries give pronunciation as well as definitions, and whenever you are in doubt you should check these. A common error is putting the wrong stress on a word, and you will find that usually the mistake is in putting the stress on the second syllable when it ought to be on the first. Examples are "ca*pit*alist" in error for "*cap*italist"; "ap*plic*able" in error for "*ap*plicable"; "com*par*able" in error for "*com*parable"; "mis*chie*vous" in error for "*mis*chievous"; and "re*mon*strate in error for "*re*monstrate".

Other errors in pronunciation are the simple result of errors in spelling, usually accompanied by a misunderstanding of the meanings of words. Your dictionary will tell you, for example, the differences between: "complaisant" and "complacent"; "palatial" and "palatal"; "allusion" and "illusion"; "perspicacity" and "perspicuity"; "mendacity" and "mendicity"; "fermentation" and "fomentation"; "ingenious" and "ingenuous"; and many others.

It will be noted from the above lists that most of the errors are made in long or relatively uncommon words. This is yet another argument in favour of using short and simple words. There is, for example, no reason why you should ever use either "mendacity" or "mendicity". The former means "lying" and the latter means "begging", and you cannot do better than use these two simpler words.

AUDIENCE REACTION AND HECKLING

A speech is made by one person and heard by others; but the processes of speaking and hearing are more closely linked than it may appear. In a good speech, the speaker and his audience are in harmony; and the task of obtaining this happy state of affairs rests with the speaker.

When you prepare your speech you will consider what sort of audience you can expect, and try to compose something that will appeal to them. However, not even the most experienced speaker can gauge exactly how the audience will react to what he has to say. Therefore, while you are speaking, observe what effect your words are having, and be ready to modify your speech accordingly as you go on.

Suppose, for example, that you have brought in a witty reference to some institution, and it has fallen very flat. This may be because it is not so witty as you thought it was; alternatively, it may be because this particular audience is unable to appreciate, or even dislikes, this sort of witticism. Now suppose that you have got a similar witticism later in the speech, and you have a strong feeling that it is going to be equally poorly received. There is only one thing to do: cut it out.

Again, you will be able to tell from the reaction of your audience whether the speech is going well generally. Yawns and whispers and half-hearted laughs and tepid applause all add up to boredom. There is only one answer to this: cut your speech short. Finish it off as quickly as you can, and sit down. Even if you do this abruptly, the effect will not be bad; on the contrary, the audience will probably now think that your speech was really better than it seemed. You will at least have obliged them by saving them from the amount of boredom they were beginning to expect. And in circumstances such as these, do not make the mistake of thinking that your listeners will get less bored as you go on. They will get more bored, unless the latter part of your speech is very different from the first part.

Heckling is rarely experienced outside political meetings, and it requires a ready wit to be put down effectively. If you are heckled, keep cool and don't lose your temper. The hecklers are trying to get your rag out, and if they succeed you will have no peace until you sit down.

The best weapon against heckling is quick wit. Without being spiteful or malicious, try to get the audience to laugh with you at the expense of the heckler. Although the hecklers make the most noise, they are usually only a small minority of the audience.

An example of brilliant repartee was given by Bernard Shaw when he made the "curtain" speech on the first night of one of his plays. The final curtain was the signal for great applause and the usual cries of "Author!" When Shaw appeared, the audience further showed its approval of the play by applauding still more loudly. Then, as the clapping and cheering died down, a single but very loud boo came down from the gallery. Shaw looked up and said: "I quite agree with you, sir—but what are we two against so many who hold a different opinion?"

HAMLET'S ADVICE

Public speaking, as has been stressed more than once, is very different from acting; but much of the advice given by Hamlet to the players can well be taken to heart by the person who has got to make a speech. Hamlet said:

"Speak the speech, I pray you, as I pronounced it to you, trippingly on the tongue; but if you mouth it, as many of your players do, I had as lief the town crier spoke my lines. Nor do not saw the air too much with your hand, thus; but use all gently: for in the very torrent, tempest, and, as I may say, the whirlwind of passion, you must acquire and beget a temperance that may give it smoothness. . . . Be not too tame neither, but let your own discretion be your tutor: suit the action to the word, the word to the action; with this special observance, that you o'erstep not the modesty of nature."

CHAPTER IV

THE CHAIRMAN'S DUTIES

THE proceedings of meetings and functions of all kinds
are invariably controlled by a chairman, who is elected
or appointed for this purpose.

A chairman should be a man of strong personality, capable of keeping order, genial and even-tempered, a fairly
able speaker who knows when to stop, and—perhaps most
important of all—a man of tact.

The duties of the chairman vary considerably according
to the nature of the meeting or function. The chairman's
duties at a company meeting lie outside the scope of this book,
and therefore these will not be discussed. For convenience
this chapter will be divided into three sections, explaining
the duties of the chairman at (1) a meeting of a club or
society; (2) a public meeting; and (3) a social dinner or other
function.

AT A MEETING OF A CLUB OR SOCIETY

The chairman's first duty is normally to have the minutes
of the last meeting read. This will usually be done by the
secretary. When the minutes have been read, it will be formally moved "That the minutes be approved". Usually this
motion will be carried unanimously, but it may happen that
a member of the meeting will question their accuracy or
raise a point at issue. The chairman must allow discussion
of this, but he must be careful also to ensure that speakers
keep strictly to the subject. A question on the minutes is
sometimes used as an excuse for discussion of a general
nature, and anything of this nature must be quickly ruled
out of order.

If an alteration in the minutes is agreed upon, it must
be made in the form of an amendment. The secretary will
insert it in its proper place and initial it.

When the meeting has formally approved the minutes
the chairman will sign them. Then he will turn to the main
business of the meeting. This may have been set out in the

form of an agenda; if so, the chairman will take the first point and continue until the whole agenda has been covered.

As the chairman introduces each subject for discussion, he has the privilege of speaking first. However, as it is part of his duty to be impartial, he will probably confine his remarks to a statement of the facts and issues. In any case his remarks should be very brief and to the point. It is important that he should set an example of brevity to the other speakers.

When a formal resolution is moved, the proposer naturally speaks first, and he is followed by the seconder. There is no fixed order of speakers in the general discussion. Each person who wants to speak has to catch the chairman's eye. It is the chairman's duty to ensure that everyone who wishes to speak has the opportunity to do so, and therefore it may be necessary to curtail lengthy speeches, especially when the speaker strays from the subject. This is where the need for tact comes in. The chairman should always try persuasion rather than enforce his authority.

The proposer of a motion has the right to speak a second time when all the other speakers have given their views. Then the question is put to the vote. This is usually recorded by a show of hands. Under the rules of most clubs and societies, in the event of an equal division of votes for and against the motion the chairman has the casting vote.

Any amendment to a motion which may be proposed must be voted on before the motion itself.

When the vote has been taken the chairman announces whether the motion is carried or not carried, and introduces the next item of business.

When the business of the meeting has been concluded, the chairman declares the meeting closed.

AT A PUBLIC MEETING

The duties of the chairman of a public meeting—for example, a political meeting—are quite simple. He merely introduces the speakers, usually with a few pleasant personal remarks.

At a party political meeting, of course, the chairman is not expected to pretend to be impartial. However, he should leave controversial questions mainly to the principal speaker or speakers, and he should never make a long speech.

Examples of speeches for the chairman at public meetings are given in Chapter IX, Speeches Nos. 47 and 48.

AT A SOCIAL DINNER OR OTHER FUNCTION

At social gatherings the chairman's functions are quite different. At a dinner his first duty is to propose the toast of the Queen. The procedure for this is explained in Chapter V, under Speech No. 1.

It will be noted in the specimen speeches that there are many other toasts that are usually proposed by the chairman. His speech in proposing such toasts is made in the same way as similar speeches by others.

Otherwise the chairman has only to call upon the other speakers, whose names and toasts will have been decided in advance. No speech of introduction is needed here. The chairman has only to say, "I now call upon Mr. —— to propose the toast of ——."

When the toast has been proposed and drunk, the chairman calls upon the responder in the same way.

When there is a musical or other entertainment, the chairman introduces each item in turn. Typical speeches for opening and closing a Smoking Concert are given in Chapter X (Speeches Nos. 74 and 75).

Chapter V

LOYAL AND PATRIOTIC TOASTS

1. THE QUEEN

THIS toast is almost always proposed by the chairman or host. It always heads the toast list; and, as smoking is not permitted until this toast has been given, the chairman is expected to propose it as soon as possible after the last course of the meal has been finished.

The proposer is not required to make a speech. He simply rises and utters the time-honoured formula:

Ladies and Gentlemen (*or* Gentlemen)—the Queen!

Immediately after this toast the chairman should announce:

Ladies and Gentlemen (*or* Gentlemen), you may smoke.

2. THE ROYAL FAMILY

This toast is much less commonly proposed. Again no speech is required, but the proposer usually gives the toast in the following form:

Ladies and Gentlemen (*or* Gentlemen),—I have the honour to propose the toast of the ... and the other members of the Royal Family.

The exact wording of this toast naturally depends on Royal Births, Marriages, and Deaths. However, there is no prescribed formula according to rank, and when the toast is to be given the chairman should ascertain the current correct form beforehand. This is issued officially from Buckingham Palace with the approval of the Queen, changes being notified as they occur.

The toasts of the Queen and the Royal Family are the only two loyal toasts that are authorized.

3. HER MAJESTY'S FORCES

(Usually proposed by the Chairman)

Hints.—Obviously there must be a patriotic ring about

this speech, but it should not be overdone and there must not be any suspicion of bombast. The proper note to strike is quiet, sober sincerity, without any striving after effect. If the proposer himself has served in the Forces, a little gentle humour may be introduced as relief, but it must not be either pompous or patronizing. If the proposer has never served in the Forces, humour is best avoided, and gratitude and respect should be expressed.

SPECIMEN

Gentlemen,—I do not think that any sailor, soldier, or airman is going to take me to task when I say that we are a peace-loving nation. Fighting is not one of our national sports. Our only conception of war is self-defence.

It is often said that it takes two to make a quarrel. I suppose there is some truth in this. A quarrelsome person has to find someone to quarrel with, and his victim is not bound to defend himself. In this sense we must plead guilty to having taken part in some long and hard quarrels in modern times. But it is worth remembering that if we had not been, in this extreme sense, such a quarrelsome nation, we should not be a nation at all today. We have a clean record. We have done everything possible to avert wars, and we have taken up arms only when our national existence and freedom have been threatened.

For a people who are so slow and reluctant to fight we have fought pretty well. I say "we", for modern war is total war, in which everyone is involved. But although the character of war has changed, let us not forget that the grim business of fighting is still done by the Fighting Forces. I do not mean to belittle the Home Front when I say that civilians, whatever their own efforts, are in the eternal debt of the men who have gone out to grapple with the enemy on land, at sea, and in the air.

Nor is this just a wartime debt. Our Forces not only win wars; they prevent them. Whatever contributions our statesmen and diplomats have made to world peace—and I think they have made many—they would have been powerless without the backing of our Armed Forces.

Our Forces are not numerically large, and they have won wars against heavy odds. Their great strength, I think, lies mainly in their efficiency and especially in their high morale.

Sane discipline is tempered with individual self-discipline, and it is this latter quality that has made our Servicemen our finest Ambassadors in every part of the world to which duty has taken them.

The toast is to Her Majesty's Forces, and I do not want to discriminate among the different Services that together protect our nation and our freedom. Our debt is the same to them all—and to them as a whole, not in parts. Yet I must mention our especial debt to those members of the Services who are professionals. Our regulars not only lead and train our citizen Servicemen; they set the standard of the Services.

Gentlemen, I give you the toast of Her Majesty's Forces; and I have pleasure in coupling with it the name of our distinguished guest, ——.

USEFUL QUOTATIONS

Nothing is more binding than the friendship of companions-in-arms.—*Hillard*.

The commonwealth of Venice in their armoury have this inscription: "Happy is that city which in time of peace thinks of war."—*Burton*.

Nothing except a battle lost can be half so melancholy as a battle won.—*Duke of Wellington*.

There never was a good war or a bad peace.—*Franklin*.

War is nothing more than a reflection or image of the soul. It is the fiend within coming out.—*Channing*.

If you want to go into battle, have an Englishman at your right hand, and another at your left, and two immediately in front and two close behind. There is something in the English which seems to guarantee security. Never forget that, even when you are most irritated by the antics of these engaging madmen.—*Voltaire*.

This England never did, nor never shall,
Lie at the proud foot of a conqueror.
Shakespeare, "King John."

He who loves not his country can love nothing.—*Lord Byron*.

Danger for danger's sake is senseless.—*Leigh Hunt*.

4. REPLY TO THE TOAST OF HER MAJESTY'S FORCES

Hints.—The reply will be made by a serving member of one of the Forces. Whatever Service he belongs to, he should stress the basic unity of the three Forces, and should also pay tribute to auxiliary Services.

SPECIMEN

Mr. Chairman, Gentlemen,—The task of replying to this most generous toast fills me with both pride and alarm. Of the two, I think the alarm is stronger. In the Army we try to keep in step, but we do not speak with one voice. Heaven forbid! But now I am called upon to speak not only for the whole of the British Army, but for the Royal Navy and the Royal Air Force as well. The task is too heavy; and I must ask you to allow me to speak simply for myself.

The first thing I want to say is that while I am dismayed at having to reply to this toast, I warmly support the form in which it has been proposed. You have honoured the three Services as one whole, and that, I think, is how they should be considered. Of course each Service has its own traditions, its own customs, and perhaps even its own language; but at heart we are pretty well at one.

I do not want to suggest that there is no such thing as inter-Service rivalry. On the contrary, it is very keen—and, I think, a good thing. Co-operation and competition are sometimes regarded as opposites, but in the Services they stimulate each other. And as for Service rivalry—well, believe me, the rivalry between the Army and the Navy or Air Force is quite tame compared with the rivalry between two of our crack regiments!

You have kindly paid tribute to those who have made one of the Services their career. As a professional, I appreciate this; but I want to ask also for your appreciation of all the other men—yes, and women—who are serving with us. There are the Volunteer Reserves and Territorials, who give up their spare time to make their valuable contribution to the defence of our land. There are the National Service youngsters, few of whom want to put on uniform, but nearly all of whom pull their weight. And there are the women's Services. We professionals have been called the hard core, but I prefer to think of us as the warp threads. For there can be no warp without weft, and no weft without warp; and when the pattern is woven, all the threads are blended into one fabric.

On behalf of this fabric, which is known as Her Majesty's Forces, I thank you.

5. THE ROYAL NAVY

(Usually proposed by the Chairman)

Hints.—Again the keynote is sober patriotism. If the proposer of the toast is serving or has served in the Army or R.A.F., he can brighten up his speech with some friendly inter-Service chaffing; but he should not overdo this, and ought to end on a note of sincere respect. If the proposer is not an ex-Serviceman, he should not try to make jokes at the expense of the Service. Historical allusions can be brought in, but should be used sparingly.

SPECIMEN

Gentlemen,—I now have the honour to propose the toast of the "Silent Service"—the Royal Navy. It may well be silent, for it has no need to boast aloud. Its deeds have always spoken for themselves. From the days of the Armada to the Battle of the Atlantic, it has held the supremacy of the sea.

The task of our Navy has been a heavy one. Not only has it had to guard our long island coastline, but it has had to protect our vital sea routes and keep them open for shipping in all the great oceans of the world. As the senior Service it has a great tradition; but at the same time it has always shown itself strikingly progressive. For many centuries naval warfare meant either ships against ships or ships against shore batteries. In modern times ships have been attacked by two new weapons of deadly striking power—one from above and one from below. Together they constituted a challenge to the very existence of the Navy—and, therefore, a challenge to the safety of our island home. Our Navy met this challenge and triumphed over it. In the Second World War it protected our lifelines when we were hardest pressed. It rescued our Army from Dunkirk; it supported the R.A.F. in the Battle of Britain; and it led the way to the liberation of Europe on D-Day. Its losses were heavy; but without it we could not have won the war. It has continued to move with the times, and if new weapons are levelled against it in the future, I am confident that it will find the answer to these as well.

Our ships are the finest in the world. But ships alone do not make a Navy. In the old days we spoke of ships of oak and hearts of oak. Nowadays our ships are of steel; and it is not too much to say that the staunchness of our sailors has evolved in a like manner with their ships. Nothing but iron courage and nerves of steel can stand the strain of naval warfare today.

Our Navy is a force of which we can be more justly proud today than ever before. I ask you, gentlemen, to drink to the health of the Royal Navy, and I couple with the toast the name of ——.

USEFUL QUOTATIONS

The best thing I know between France and England is the sea.—*Jerrold*.

A new recruit, on putting to sea and suffering with sickness, said afterwards that for the first day he was afraid he would die, and the second day he was afraid he wouldn't.

Thank God, I have done my duty.—*Nelson's last words*.
See also under Her Majesty's Forces.

6. REPLY TO THE TOAST OF THE ROYAL NAVY
SPECIMEN

Mr. Chairman, Gentlemen,—I must apologize for standing up and breaking one of the naval traditions which has just been warmly praised. I have been reminded that the Service to which I have the honour of belonging is famous for its silence; and such a compliment deserves a more appropriate reply than a speech.

Nor, indeed, is there anything I can say, beyond expressing my thanks for the most cordial way in which you have received this toast. I would add only this: service in the British Navy is a great privilege as well as a responsibility. In playing our part in the defence of the country we have always known that we have had the trust and confidence of the people behind us. This means a lot to us; and, come what may, I promise you that we shall continue to try to be worthy of this trust. Gentlemen, on behalf of the Navy, I thank you.

7. THE BRITISH ARMY

(Usually proposed by the Chairman).
Hints.—See under The Royal Navy.

SPECIMEN

Gentlemen,—Khaki is not a glamorous colour, and glamour is not a word that comes to mind when you think of soldiers. Of the three Services, the Army is probably the least showy and spectacular. But it is certainly not the least necessary or the least deserving of our admiration. Even in the atomic age, warfare is still fundamentally territorial. The Second World War was fought with torpedoes and mines, bombs and rockets, and all manner of fiendish weapons used at sea and in the air; but the final victory was won on land—by the British and Allied Armies.

We have reason to be proud of our Army, although it exists, as it were, in spite of our natural inclinations. We are not a militarily minded nation. We do not glory in regimentation. To the average young Briton, putting on a uniform is at the best an unfortunate necessity. Military service is simply a duty, to be performed with a maximum of efficiency and a minimum of fuss.

To foreigners our soldiers must appear deceptively harmless. They do not boast or strut or bully. Nowhere in the world can you find troops more modest and restrained in the hour of victory or more decent in their general behaviour. But put these same men in a tight corner—and our Armies have been in many tight corners—and they reveal an ability to fight against superior odds that is unique among the Armies of the world. The British, it has been said, never know when they are beaten; and it is only the refusal of the British Army to admit defeat that has saved this nation many times.

Efficiency and fitness, sane but not harsh discipline, initiative and respect for authority, courage and daring and endurance—these are some of the qualities of our soldiers. But there is another quality which does not belong to individuals. It is team spirit—a part of the British character, and nowhere more characteristic than in the British Army.

Gentlemen, I give you the toast of our Army, coupled with the name of ——.

USEFUL QUOTATIONS

I don't know what effect these men may have on the enemy, but, by Gad, they frighten me!—*Duke of Wellington, inspecting his troops before Waterloo.*

We're in the Final now.—*Unknown British soldier after the evacuation from Dunkirk in* 1940.

See also under Her Majesty's Forces.

8. REPLY TO THE TOAST OF THE BRITISH ARMY
SPECIMEN

Mr. Chairman, Gentlemen,—I wish to thank you most sincerely for the way you have accepted this toast. As a professional soldier I find it heartening to hear such kind words from one of my employers, and I am glad to think that you do not consider that you get such bad value for the considerable amount of money that we cost you. I am glad too that you have not clothed the military machine with any false glamour. I will tell you frankly that we know we are, at best, only a necessary evil. We produce nothing, we consume a lot, and we cost a good deal. We occupy valuable ground, we take up housing accommodation, we have to be clothed and fed, and we can offer nothing in return unless the country happens to be in danger of attack.

I have been told, very properly, that we are not a militarist nation, and it is worth remembering that peace-time conscription is still quite a recent thing in this country. It was not adopted from choice, but from necessity, and any comment on its desirability or otherwise is out of date. But I should like to say this about our National Service youngsters. They are, for the most part, a fine set of lads, and whatever their feelings, they do their job thoroughly and conscientiously. It is not for me to talk about the effect of military service on them; but whatever else it does, I think the Army at least gives them an idea of comradeship and team spirit that is not entirely without value.

Gentlemen, on behalf of the Army, I thank you for your generous welcome to this toast.

9. THE ROYAL AIR FORCE

(Usually proposed by the Chairman)

Never in the field of human conflict was so much owed by so many to so few.—*Winston Churchill.*

Hints.—See also under The Royal Navy.

SPECIMEN

Gentlemen,—Our nation is steeped in tradition, and nowhere is this more apparent than in the Armed Forces. Both our Navy and Army have long and glorious histories. The history of our Air Force is much shorter—but certainly not less glorious. It has shown that tradition does not depend on antiquity—for, young as it is, the R.A.F. already has established its own distinctive tradition. (It has even established its own distinctive language, too!)

This country has had to fight many critical battles in order to remain free. Some of these have become epics in our history. The Navy had its Trafalgar; the Army had its Waterloo; and the R.A.F. had the Battle of Britain. In each of these battles the enemy fought with superior strength; in each it seemed that only a miracle could save us.

The Battle of Britain was fought and won by young men, and when we think of the R.A.F. we think almost instinctively of youth—of youthful energy and daring and amazing courage. The R.A.F. is older now, but the spirit of service seems unchanged.

While we hope and pray for peace, we must preserve our defences; and I do not think it is any exaggeration to say that a strong Air Force is our best guarantee for peace.

Gentlemen, I give you the toast of the Royal Air Force —coupled with the name of ——.

USEFUL QUOTATIONS

See under Her Majesty's Forces.

10. REPLY TO THE TOAST OF THE ROYAL AIR FORCE

SPECIMEN

Mr. Chairman, Gentlemen,—I feel quite unworthy of the honour of replying to this toast. My only qualification is my youth.

I am not going to pretend that I am not proud of belonging to the R.A.F. You, sir, have spoken of it as a young Service, and compared with the Navy and the Army I know it is. But to me it has an almost venerable history which will take a lot of living up to.

I know that we have the reputation of being a bit harebrained, but I want to assure you that we take our flying seriously. Perhaps that is why we run a bit wild when we come down to earth! And I want to add one more thing. Most people, when they think of the R.A.F., think only of aircrew. I ask you to spare a thought for those who keep us in the air—the ground staff who look after the aircraft and make flying safe. Their work is hard and monotonous, and all too often it goes unappreciated—by the public, at least. But it is appreciated by the aircrew. Our lives depend on the efficiency of the ground staff—and we live to be grateful to them.

On behalf of the Royal Air Force, gentlemen, I thank you for the welcome you have given to this toast.

11. THE COUNTY REGIMENT
(Usually proposed by the Chairman)

Hints.—See under Her Majesty's Forces. The appeal will, of course, be of a local nature.

SPECIMEN

Gentlemen,—In these days of centralization, a county does not mean as much as it did once. I am not going to discuss whether that is a good or a bad thing; but I must say that I think it would be a very bad thing if county divisions disappeared altogether. Fortunately we can be sure that this will never happen. The M.C.C. would not allow it.

Nor, I think, would the War Office allow such a thing to happen without putting up a strong resistance. And, gentlemen, as you know, there are no more stubborn defenders of last ditches than the Whitehall warriors! But they are shrewd as well as stubborn, and they know the value of local patriotism. When a man joins the Army he becomes a number—but his Regiment has a name. Our County Regiment has not only a name, but a most honourable history. You know of its famous exploits of the distant past, and especially of the more recent past; and I know that nobody will challenge me when I say that its record will stand comparison with that of any other Regiment in the Army.

If you read the history of the County Regiment—and it is a wonderful story—you will find a certain continuity in it. The Regiment has served in many different parts of the world; it has fought many kinds of actions; it has fought with various sorts of weapons and, of course, it has had several generations of soldiers. Yet in every action it has acquitted itself with the same qualities of courage and dash, grit and determination. I am not suggesting that these qualities are given at birth to everyone who is lucky enough to be born in our county; but I do say that they are traditional in the County Regiment, and they are the first things that every new recruit learns to appreciate.

I know you all share my hope that our Regiment will not have to fight another action. It can afford to rest on its laurels, and it is our hope that it will be allowed to do so. But if it ever has to be tested again—well, we know that it will again make the name of our county resound all over the land.

Gentlemen, I give you the toast of the Royal —— Regiment, and I couple with it the name of Colonel ——.

USEFUL QUOTATIONS

See under Her Majesty's Forces *and* The British Army.

12. REPLY TO THE TOAST OF THE COUNTY REGIMENT

SPECIMEN

Gentlemen,—I am proud to be able to reply to the toast of the Regiment that I have the honour to command. It is an honour, gentlemen, and I am always conscious of it. Our Regiment has had such able and distinguished commanding officers in the past—I need only to mention Colonel —— and Colonel ——, that I can hardly hope to live up to the standard they have set. But fortunately our Regiment does not depend on its C.O. I might almost say that it commands itself; for while we pride ourselves on discipline, we have yet more reason to be proud of the magnificent self-discipline shown by all ranks. It is my firm belief that we have the finest officers, the finest N.C.O.s, and the finest men in the whole British Army. With such a composition, gentlemen, a Regiment can triumph over everything, including an indifferent C.O.

We have just been told that the county is proud of the Regiment; and I must assure you that the Regiment is very proud of the county. It not only gives us our name; it binds us together. It means that if we are again called upon to fight to defend England, we shall be fighting together to defend the same part of England, which we all hold so dear.

On behalf of the——, gentlemen, thank you.

13. THE ROYAL NAVAL VOLUNTEER RESERVE
(Usually proposed by the Chairman)

Hints.—See under The Royal Navy *and* The Territorials.

SPECIMEN

Gentlemen,—It is my privilege tonight to propose the toast of the Royal Naval Volunteer Reserve. This is not a very common toast, because usually the R.N.V.R. is included in the more general toast to the Royal Navy. I know that members of the Reserve are happy to be thought of as part of the Navy, and I know equally well that the Navy is proud to include their company. Whatever praise our Navy deserves—and it can hardly be praised too highly—is due equally to the Volunteer Reserve.

These two words tell the whole story. On the one hand, it is a voluntary service, and its members give their time and effort—often at the cost of personal sacrifice—to help in the vital work of safeguarding our country. On the other hand it is a Reserve, which means that it is liable to be called to full-time duty only when such duty is likely to be most arduous and dangerous. It follows from these definitions that every member of the R.N.V.R. is a man of high patriotism, in the finest sense of the word; capable of genuine self-sacrifice; and of real courage. If he did not possess these qualities he would never have joined the Reserve.

I do not need to remind you of the work of the R.N.V.R. in two World Wars. The deeds of the Service are enshrined in the history of the Royal Navy. And if ever these gallant volunteers are called upon for a similar task—though Heaven forbid!—then we know that they will serve with the same spirit as they have done in the past.

Gentlemen, I give you the toast of the Royal Naval Volunteer Reserve, coupled with the name of——.

USEFUL QUOTATIONS

See under The Royal Navy *and* Her Majesty's Forces.

14. REPLY TO THE TOAST OF THE ROYAL NAVAL VOLUNTEER RESERVE

SPECIMEN

Mr. Chairman, Gentlemen,—The Royal Navy is called the Silent Service, and I should hate to think of this high tradition of the professionals being disgraced by an amateur like me. All I can say in reply to your very generous toast is that we are proud to belong, in a small way, to the Navy itself. We do not deserve the particular compliments you have paid us, for service in the Reserve involves no real hardship and offers great rewards. It is, as you say, a voluntary service, which means that we are in it because we want to be; and I can assure you that we want to be in it because we like it.

On behalf of the R.N.V.R. I thank you for the cordial welcome you have given to this toast.

15. THE TERRITORIALS
(Usually proposed by the Chairman)

Hints.—At a function given specially for a unit of the Territorial Army this toast is, of course, of great importance.

It may be proposed also at a more general civic function or at a purely social function which happens to be attended by a fair number of Territorials. The toast at the social function should be proposed in a lighter and less formal way; but whatever the occasion, the speaker should bring in the local as well as the national aspect of the Territorial Army. *See also under* The Royal Navy.

SPECIMEN

Gentlemen,—I do not think any Regular soldier is likely to quarrel with me when I say that the nation could not get on without the Territorial Army. I hesitate to say that without the Territorials we could not have survived, for the phrase is greatly overworked and in this century we have several times been in circumstances in which survival was theoretically impossible. But I can say with certainty that our survival and our continued freedom and prosperity owe a great deal to this volunteer army of ours.

Patriotism is a word that has been often abused, and the term "a great patriot" is sometimes applied to men whose love of their country has been professed only in words. It should be reserved for those who are prepared to make personal sacrifices; and I do not think it is any exaggeration to say that every man who joins the Territorials is a great patriot. He volunteers for a service that brings him no financial or material reward; that may cause him considerable inconvenience; and that certainly makes substantial demands on his leisure time. He does this in the full knowledge that in the event of war, he will be called upon to stand up to the first onslaught by the aggressor, while a citizen army is created and trained behind the lines.

In two world wars our Territorial Army has had to carry out this task, and each time it has done it with valour and efficiency. We all hope that it will be spared a further sacrifice of this sort; and it is our best guarantee against such a tragedy that our Territorial Army should be strong, well trained, and well equipped. The need for the Territorials has in no way decreased since the introduction of compulsory National Service.

We have national pride in our Territorial Army, and a civic pride in our own —— (name the local Territorial unit).

We owe it to these fine lads to express our pride in the form of practical gratitude.

Gentlemen, I ask you to drink to the health of the Territorial Army, coupling with it the names of —— and ——.

USEFUL QUOTATIONS

See under Her Majesty's Forces *and* The British Army.

16. REPLY TO THE TOAST OF THE TERRITORIALS

SPECIMEN

Mr. Chairman, Gentlemen,—I feel greatly honoured to reply to this toast, which has been proposed in such generous terms. But I hope you will not think I am being discourteous when I venture to contradict one statement that has been made about us. You, sir, have said that our service brings no reward. We think it does.

It is often said that we British are not a militarily minded nation, and certainly not even the most ferocious Terriers have any taste for war; but we have a taste for sport and other outdoor activities; we enjoy a fortnight under canvas; and, above all, we enjoy our comradeship together and the knowledge that we are doing something useful with our spare time.

Nor are we out of pocket on the deal. Certainly the sums of money that we receive for our service are small—but think of the money we save! When I think of what an ordinary fortnight's holiday costs, and compare the enjoyment of it with what we get out of our annual camp, I count myself lucky to be in the Territorials. So, while we appreciate your support, please don't think of us as martyrs. We thoroughly enjoy our life in the Territorials, and if there is anyone here who wants to find a good way of using his spare time without having to pay for the pleasure, I strongly recommend him to join us.

On behalf of the Territorial Army, and of the —— (unit) in particular, I thank you for the way in which you have received this toast.

17. OUR NOBLE SELVES

(A toast to a particular Regiment, Battery, or Squadron)

Hints.—This toast, which is used at a reunion where no outsiders are present, is generally proposed by the chairman. While the speech must have a ring of sincerity, it can be pleasantly informal, and the speaker should try to evoke happy memories of old comradeship.

SPECIMEN

Gentlemen,—It is my great privilege to propose the toast of the finest unit in the British Army. Of course I do not need to say which unit I am speaking of. I know it was the finest unit when I served in it. I believe it was the finest unit before I served in it. And I am sure that many of my old comrades will be quick to tell me that it cannot help but be even finer now that I am out of it!

Old soldiers, I know, are expected to fade away. I am happy to say that I see no sign of any fading here tonight. On the contrary, unless my memory fails me, it seems to me that most of the old soldiers whom I knew when they were younger are now looming larger than ever.

Not all of us here tonight served in the ——th at the same time. Not all of us have the same memories. No doubt some of the most stirring deeds that took place in my time have failed to be passed down to the next generation. It is even possible that the present members of the unit have never heard of (here insert a reference to a humorous incident connected with someone present at the function), or of (insert another similar reference). If these things have been forgotten, then I feel I am at least serving some purpose in recalling them.

Gentlemen, I am not going to bang a drum in praise of the ——th. It does not need it. We have never advertised our glories to outsiders, and we do not have to advertise them to ourselves. We have a great history, and I am sure that we have a great future. Before I close, I must ask you to think of our proudest but saddest possession: our roll of honour. It includes names that are familiar to most of us— names of men whom we should like to have here tonight. Let us pay homage to them, above all, as we drink—to the ——th!

USEFUL QUOTATIONS

See under Her Majesty's Forces *and* The British Army.

18. THE WOMEN'S SERVICES

(Usually proposed by a member of H.M. Forces)

Hints.—This is a general toast, like the toast to Her Majesty's Forces; toasts to the particular branches of the Women's Services are given on the following pages. All these toasts are invariably given by men, usually by members of the Forces. The keynote of each speech should be appreciation of the work women do, and the speaker must be careful to avoid any hint of patronage or condescension.

SPECIMEN

Ladies and Gentlemen,—Serving one's country, like voting, used to be a man's job alone. The women's job was to keep the home fires burning; and if it had been left to the men, that is all they would still be doing. For no one can say that the men dragged them out of their homes, any more than it could be said that women were dragged to the polls. The Women's Services came into being as a result of the demand of the women themselves. That demand was conceded rather grudgingly, and with many shakings of heads, by men who were convinced in advance that women would never make soldiers.

I do not need to remind you of the way in which the Women's Services have proved themselves. They served with great distinction in two world wars, and their heroic work in the Mixed Batteries and in other fields is now a part of military history.

Many Servicemen were inclined at first to think of their probable value as mainly ornamental. Please don't misunderstand me—I should be the last person to underrate their decorative qualities! But we soon found that they had not come merely to brighten up the lives of the troops. They were in uniform to do a job of work, and the way they did their job won the admiration of us all. After the First World War the Women's Services were stood down. They returned for the Second World War, and made themselves so indispensable that they now have permanent peacetime establishments. They have won their colours the hard way, and now the men of the Forces are proud to acknowledge them as their comrades in uniform..

Ladies and gentlemen, I ask you to join me in this salute to the gallant women—I should prefer to call them ladies, but they would not allow it—of the Services!

USEFUL QUOTATIONS

The female woman is one of the greatest institutions of which this land can boast.—*Artemus Ward*.

Great women belong to history and to self-sacrifice.—*Leigh Hunt*.

Nature was in earnest when she made women.—*O. W. Holmes*.

See also under Her Majesty's Forces *and* The Ladies.

19. REPLY TO THE TOAST OF THE WOMEN'S SERVICES
SPECIMEN

Ladies and Gentlemen,—Thank you for the kind way in which you have received this toast. I would almost suspect you of flattery—and being a woman, I should not seriously object to that—were it not for the fact that in my Service life I have had so many proofs of the goodwill of the men's Services. It is true, I agree, that we had to demand to be allowed to share in the defence of our country, but I do not think that the early objections were based entirely on the grounds that have been suggested. Rather, it was man's natural instinct of chivalry that wanted to spare us from possible hardship and danger.

It is not surprising that we get on so well with the men's Services. As you know, there's something about a soldier; all the nice girls love a sailor; while those R.A.F. types are simply irresistible! Co-operation with the men's Services has often been so close that it has ended at the altar. Did I say ended? That was the last thing I meant.

I must say how much we appreciate the way in which the men take us seriously, trust us to do our jobs, and let us get on with them. Please do not think that we imagine that our contribution is, or can ever be, equal to that of the men who have to go out and fight; but we are proud to do our bit alongside those who protect our land.

On behalf of the Women's Services, I thank you.

20. THE WOMEN'S ROYAL ARMY CORPS

(Usually proposed by a member of the Army)
Hints.—See under The Women's Services.

SPECIMEN

Ladies and Gentlemen,—Before I ask you to join me in this very important toast, I want to tell you a very short—and true—story about two young soldiers. One of them was a handsome, dashing young fellow who greatly fancied himself as a lady-killer. The other was a more serious lad, who had no girl-friends, and described himself as a confirmed bachelor and even a woman-hater.

These two soldiers were serving in the same unit, and one day they heard the news that they were to be reinforced by members of the Women's Royal Army Corps. The lady-killer was delighted. "Just what we need," he said with an anticipatory gleam in his eyes. The woman-hater threw up his hands in despair. "At least I thought I should be safe from *that* in the Army," he complained.

A month later the two soldiers exchanged opinions again. The lady-killer looked more subdued, and even a little crest-fallen. "These girls are useless—they don't know what they're here for," he grumbled. His comrade, who had lost his despair, answered thoughtfully: "Oddly enough, that's just what they do know."

The moral, I think, is clear enough; but just to make it clear that the girls are more human than our lady-killer thought, I had better add that within three months of their arrival, the woman-hater married one of them!

The genius of the Women's Royal Army Corps is that its members have such a keen appreciation of the old army distinction between conduct on and off parade. When they are on duty they are hard-working, efficient soldiers; off duty, they are human, feminine, and wholly charming.

You all know what these girls did during the war. In those days, when many of them shared soldiers' dangers in Mixed Batteries, they were called Auxiliaries. They proved themselves a good deal more than that, and they have deservedly become an Army Corps in their own right.

Ladies and gentlemen, I ask you to drink to the health of the Women's Royal Army Corps, and with this toast I couple the name of ——.

USEFUL QUOTATIONS

See under The Women's Services *and* The Ladies.

21. REPLY TO THE TOAST OF THE WOMEN'S ROYAL ARMY CORPS

SPECIMEN

Ladies and Gentlemen,—Thank you for your kindness. You have, I think, honoured us too highly. We are proud of our Service, but conscious of our limitations. As members of an independent Corps in the British Army, we try to be good soldiers—but we are still women. I don't think we are frail women, though. Some of us might have been as recruits, but it didn't last. Yet the jobs we can do are limited, and in the most dangerous and arduous work of the soldier we cannot compete with the men.

Fortunately we do not have to compete, because the men are so co-operative. We are allotted our spheres, and left to get on with the job without interference. Many of us serve in mixed units, and then we work hand in hand with the men. Have I said the wrong thing? I don't mean to imply that the men have to hold our hands—oh, dear, now I've got into a worse mess, but you know what I mean!

On behalf of the Corps, thank you.

22. THE WOMEN'S ROYAL NAVAL SERVICE

(Usually proposed by a member of the Royal Navy)

Hints.—See under The Women's Services. *See also* the specimen toast of The Women's Royal Army Corps; the opening story about the two soldiers can be adapted by changing " soldiers " to " sailors."

SPECIMEN

Ladies and Gentlemen,—Britannia, whom we tell to rule the waves, is a lady; and according to her picture on the back of a penny, a very warlike lady too. Our picture of a Wren is less fierce—although this may be deceptive—and a good deal more charming. But then the Wrens do not try to rule the waves. They simply keep the men who sail over them in order.

The Navy has the honour of being the senior Service and the reputation of being the most hidebound in tradition. This reputation is a bit exaggerated. According to some popular views, you might think that most sailors are still bewailing the days of the windjammers and complaining about this new-fangled idea of steam. But it is true that the Navy has its roots deep in the past, and traditions of the Service die hard. Yet no tradition died so quickly as the idea that the place of women was in the home—or rather in the next port. The Wrens came; we saw them; and they conquered.

Please do not mistake me about the nature of their conquest. It was not merely a case of sailors falling for a pretty face after staring at each other's ugly mugs out at sea. Not that we don't get tired of each other's mugs—and not that the Wrens' faces aren't pretty. But I don't need to tell you that here! Yet the real reason why the Wrens won our salt-stained hearts was that they were doing a job of work in what I can only call a sailor-like fashion. It was not just that they were efficient—although they certainly were; it was not just that they worked hard and took their service seriously— although they did. But in a way that was almost uncanny, they grasped the very spirit of the Navy right from the beginning, and became part of it almost as if they had always belonged. It was this that made it so easy for us to accept and appreciate them; and now it is hard indeed to think of the Navy without them.

Ladies and gentlemen—to the Wrens, God bless em!

USEFUL QUOTATIONS

See under The Women's Services *and* The Ladies.

23. REPLY TO THE TOAST OF THE WOMEN'S ROYAL NAVAL SERVICE

SPECIMEN

Ladies and Gentlemen,—Pride, I know, is a dangerous thing, but I must tell you frankly that I have never got over my pride in belonging to the Wrens. I don't think any of us have. Britain is a seafaring nation, and the glories of our Navy reach the hearts of British women as well as men.

Please don't think that we imagine ourselves the successors of the great sailor-heroes of our history. We know that our own part in the service of the Navy is very small. But the fact that we have a part at all is to us a great privilege and honour. Most important of all is the recognition that we get from the Navy itself. I only hope we shall always be worthy of the Service.

On behalf of the Wrens, ladies and gentlemen, I thank you most sincerely.

24. THE WOMEN'S ROYAL AIR FORCE

(Usually proposed by a member of the Royal Air Force)

Hints.—*See under* The Women's Services. *See also* the specimen toast of The Women's Royal Army Corps; the opening story about the two soldiers can be adapted by changing "soldiers" to "airmen".

SPECIMEN

Ladies and Gentlemen,—nothing gives me greater pleasure than to propose the health of the Women's Royal Air Force. I should like to give you a little talk entitled "W.R.A.F.'s whom I have met"—and believe me, I have met some stunning types; but I understand that this would not be quite in accordance with my present duties. The Women's Royal Air Force, as various of its members have told me several times, does not exist for the solace and entertainment of the R.A.F. That is, as it were, a by-product of its function. Its real purpose is to do a job of work.

Now let me stop fooling and tell you that we really do appreciate the work these girls do. Please don't get the idea they are just glorified air hostesses. Many of them are highly trained and highly skilled technicians, and when we go up in the air our safety depends on them. You may rest assured that we have full confidence in their ability and their sense of responsibility. They do not let us down—they keep us up!

So even if they did not have feminine hearts beating beneath their smart uniforms—even if they had no social value at all—they would still be invaluable. Having made this clear, perhaps you will allow me to add that I rejoice in the fact that when they are off duty they are very charming girls.

Ladies and gentlemen, I ask you to drink to the health of the Women's Royal Air Force, and I couple with this toast the name of ——.

USEFUL QUOTATIONS

See under The Women's Services *and* The Ladies.

25. REPLY TO THE TOAST OF THE WOMEN'S ROYAL AIR FORCE

SPECIMEN

Ladies and Gentlemen,—Thank you very much for the reception you have given to this toast. As you know, we used to be called auxiliaries; and it was only after the Second World War that we were made into a Service in our own right. I hope you will not think that this has made us get above ourselves. Whatever our name, we know that our function now is the same as it was during the days when the R.A.F. was fighting the Battle of Britain—to help the men who fly.

The whole nation is rightly proud of the glorious achievements of the R.A.F. Everyone knows our debt to the Service. I hope you will not blame us if we bask a little in reflected glory. We do not overrate our contribution to the war effort, but we did have the privilege of serving with the R.A.F. when it was most severely tested. If we did just a little to help them—and we like to think we did—then we are immensely proud of it.

The proposer of this toast has said some kind things about us, and not only from the strictly Service point of view. He has reminded you that we are women, with all the feminine faults and failings. But I think you will have gathered from his remarks that the R.A.F. does take us seriously, and this makes our work worth while. So long as the R.A.F. thinks that we are worth having, then we shall go on doing our best.

On behalf of the Women's Royal Air Force, thank you very much.

26. THE NURSING SERVICES

Hints.—Simple admiration is the keynote of this speech, and the praise should be sincere rather than extravagant.

SPECIMEN

Ladies and Gentlemen,—I have great pleasure in proposing the toast of the Nursing Services. This toast hardly needs a speech, for our debt to the Nursing Services is too well known. Nursing the sick is service in its highest form— service involving hard work and bringing little material reward. It demands unselfishness, a will to work, and above all a sense of vocation.

Our nurses are our heroines in peace and war. They receive few decorations. All too often they are taken for granted. While we rightly revere the name of Florence Nightingale, we are all too apt to overlook the fact that the tradition of the "Lady with the Lamp" is still carried on. The name of Edith Cavell conjures up a picture of unique courage and devotion to duty in the highest sense of the words—and courage and devotion to duty are integral parts of the very spirit of the Nursing Services today.

Our nurses prefer to carry out their tasks anonymously, and they seek no praise. I shall not embarrass them further. Ladies and gentlemen, I ask you to drink to the health of the Nursing Services, and I couple with this toast the name of Sister ——.

USEFUL QUOTATIONS

See under The Women's Services *and* The Ladies.

27. REPLY TO THE TOAST OF THE NURSING SERVICES

SPECIMEN

Ladies and Gentlemen.—Thank you for the kind welcome you have given to this toast. Really I think it was too kind, for we nurses are very ordinary beings. I am not going to pretend that nursing is not hard work, or that we don't sometimes find it tedious; but by and large we do it because we like it, and that seems a good reason for doing any job. For anyone who didn't like the work I imagine it would be pretty hateful; but for our part we count ourselves to be doing something that appeals to us.

And I must add a word about our patients. I expect that most of you will have been in our hands at some time or other, so I can make it quite personal when I say that for the most part we like our patients. There are a few exceptions, of course—and in my experience the biggest grumblers are the ones who have the least wrong with them. Many of the most seriously ill cases that I have nursed have shown such appreciation and good humour that it was a positive joy to do what little I could to ease their suffering. For although a doctor, and especially a surgeon, may have to consider the disease more than the patient, for us nurses sickness is a very human matter; and I know of no finer sight in the world than a sick person smiling bravely in spite of suffering. It is that sort of sight that makes nursing really worth while.

On behalf of the Nursing Services, ladies and gentlemen, thank you.

CHAPTER VI

CIVIC TOASTS

28. THE MAYOR AND CORPORATION

Hints.—This toast is generally proposed at a civic dinner or other function, where the Mayor will be known personally by many of those present. A personal element should therefore be introduced into the speech—for example, if it is known that the Mayor is a keen golfer, some humorous reference should be made to the fact.

SPECIMEN

Mr. Chairman, Gentlemen,—I am happy to have the duty of proposing the toast of the Mayor and Corporation. Most of us, I am afraid, are in the habit of taking the Corporation for granted. What is worse, on the few occasions when we do think about it, our thoughts are not always kindly. We remember the Corporation when there are elections—and then, of course, the Corporation remembers us; and we remember it especially twice every year, when we get the demands for our rates. Otherwise we seem to forget that the Corporation exists. My only defence for this apparently ungrateful attitude is that it shows, far better than any words could do, just how efficiently the Corporation does its work. It never lets us down.

But although we may take the Corporation for granted, the same does not apply to the Mayor. He is not the sort of man you can ignore. He is a personality—a character. He leaves his mark on everything he does. If you do not believe me, I invite you to go up to the golf course and have a look at the bunker behind the green at the fifteenth hole. There you will see what a worshipful niblick did three months ago.

But I am not being fair. Our Mayor, as you know, is tireless in the performance of his many public duties, and we have every reason to be grateful to him. Both he and all the members of the Corporation labour unstintingly for the good of the community. They set a magnificent example in local government—and I only wish that the Governments of the world were in similar hands.

Gentlemen, I ask you to drink to the health of our Mayor and Corporation.

29. REPLY TO THE TOAST OF THE MAYOR AND CORPORATION

SPECIMEN

Mr. Chairman, Gentlemen,—You are very kind—much kinder than we deserve. We of the Corporation are not particularly modest folk, but I am sure my colleagues will want me to say that we have not earned all your compliments. For the fact is that we do comparatively little. The real work is done by the various officers who put local government into effect. I know that the standard of local government in this country is exceptionally high, but I am convinced that it is nowhere higher than it is here. Why, they even manage to collect the rates!

But I fear I am doing an injustice to my colleagues. They do work—really hard. The only person at the Town Hall who is idle is myself. This may surprise you—I hope it does, for I have always tried to look busy—but it will not surprise you more than it did me when I assumed office. I will tell you frankly that I had been dreading the day, wondering how on earth I could carry out all the numerous duties that would be expected of me. Groundless fears; the duties were there, all right—but the work was done for me.

Therefore, gentlemen, it is with some pangs of conscience on my own behalf—but not on behalf of my colleagues— that I thank you most sincerely for the cordial reception you have given to this toast.

30. HER MAJESTY'S JUDGES

Hints.—The task of proposing this toast is usually given to an experienced speaker. The speech needs to be good, with some real wit, because the reply will almost certainly be an example of good oratory. Humour is essential here.

SPECIMEN

Gentlemen,—The task of proposing this toast fills me with alarm. This is not because I am frightened of Her Majesty's Judges in general—certainly not through any particular fear of Mr. Justice——, whom we are so happy to see here tonight. For by a fortunate chance Mr. Justice —— is one of Her Majesty's Judges who has never had to pass judgment on me. I do not fear him for his power—yet I fear him for another reason. He will reply to this toast; you may be sure you will hear a speech of great wit and eloquence, which will make my present effort seem even feebler than it is.

There is a common belief in this country that Judges are rather dry, inhuman men, who live apart in a world of torts and malfeasances, and really have little idea of everyday life as the rest of us know it. Many Judges, of course, deliberately foster this idea. For hours they sit in silence, apparently unmoved by either the eloquence of the barristers or the pathos and drama of the evidence of witnesses. You wonder if they are really alive. Then, when you have almost given up hope, the Judge leans forward and, with a slightly puzzled frown, asks some such question as: "Who is Charles Chaplin?"

This almost unbelievable ignorance—and I am stretching a point when I say that it is only *almost* unbelievable—contrasts strangely with the omniscience of the barristers. They know everything about everything. One day a barrister is speaking with all the authority of an economist; the next day he is arguing equally impressively on the proper way to prune roses.

Now as Judges would have us believe that they know nothing about economics or pruning roses, one may wonder what they were doing before they were elevated to their high office. Where did they come from? The answer, as you know, is that they came from the Bar. Please do not misunderstand me. The Bar I am speaking of is a very dry one—dry as dust, in fact—with so much dust that the barristers even find enough to try to throw into the eyes of the jury. So that a Judge who now professes ignorance even of the existence of Charles Chaplin was himself once an expert on economics, horticulture, and every other subject that comes the way of a barrister.

The explanation for this change is not so difficult to find.

A Barrister and a Judge have only one thing in common: knowledge of the law. In at least one vitally important respect they are utterly different. The Barrister prosecutes or pleads. He is frankly partisan. The Judge is impartial. That, I think, is why a Judge becomes a different person from the man who used to be a Barrister.

Be that as it may, I am sure you will all agree with me when I say that Her Majesty's Judges enjoy not only our respect and admiration, but our confidence. There is no rough justice in this country, and no innocent man needs to fear wrongful conviction.

Gentlemen, I have great pleasure in asking you to drink the health of Her Majesty's Judges, and I couple with this toast the name of Mr. Justice ——.

USEFUL QUOTATIONS

For pity is the virtue of the law,
And none but tyrants use it cruelly.—*Shakespeare*.
The law hath not been dead, though it hath slept.—*Shakespeare*.

31. THE MAGISTRATES

Hints.—This speech does not call for the same standard of oratory as the toast of Her Majesty's Judges, and a more personal element may be introduced if the magistrates present are well known to the speaker and his audience.

SPECIMEN

Gentlemen,—I have a vague recollection from my school-days that when I had finished learning the dozen different ways of expressing the Latin for a table, I was put on to declining a noun called "magister". I believe that it is from this word that "magistrate" comes; and I know that it means "master".

This seems very appropriate, for in the presence of a magistrate I feel very much like a schoolboy in the presence of his master. Indeed, if I remember rightly we used to refer to our Head as "the beak".

By quite extraordinary and sustained good fortune, I have not yet been brought before our magistrates. I expect this will surprise you; it is a constant source of amazement to me. But when my day does come—as I fear it must—I invite you all to come to court and hear what the clerk says when he is asked if I am "known".

Perhaps because of my lack of knowledge of the magistrates in their official capacity, I am very happy to propose their health. The Bench is held in deservedly high esteem, and I am sure you will agree with me when I say that we are particularly lucky in this respect. Gentlemen, the magistrates.

USEFUL QUOTATIONS

See under Her Majesty's Judges.

32. REPLY TO THE TOAST OF THE MAGISTRATES

SPECIMEN

Gentlemen,—It is a novel and refreshing experience for me to receive such cordial good wishes for my health in public. More commonly I hear expressions of hope for my early demise. From the cordial reception you have given to this toast I can only conclude that you all have very clear consciences and that none of you expect to appear before the Bench. May I offer you my congratulations and, in return, express my hope that you will all continue to keep clear of the Law.

If, however, you contemplate a life of crime, it would seem that now is an excellent time to start. You are well aware, I am sure, that magistrates are crusty folk and that the severity of the sentences they impose depends mainly on their physical well-being and the state of their livers. My criminal friends assure me that it is always better after lunch, provided that the lunch was a good one. All magistrates are bad, of course; but a well-fed magistrate is not so bad as a hungry one. A liverish magistrate is the worst of all.

At the moment I am extremely well fed, and I certainly shouldn't have the heart to send any of my fellow-diners to the galleys. But I must give you a warning. If you decide to crack a crib or park your car on the wrong side of the road, or commit some other equally heinous offence, I urge you to do it as quickly as possible and, if you are caught—as you will be, of course—to insist on an immediate appearance in Court. If you wait till tomorrow morning you will certainly find me suffering from indigestion and very liverish.

So far I have been speaking only on my own behalf. But your toast was to the Bench as a whole, and on behalf of my fellow magistrates I must speak more cautiously. I know that they would want me to express my appreciation of your hearty good wishes, because I know that they share my view that those who are privileged to assist in the administration of the Law should try to earn the goodwill of the community that the Law is designed to protect. British justice is something that we can all be proud of, and one of the reasons for our pride is that the magistrates have strictly limited powers. In some countries a magistrate is regarded with fear by the innocent as well as the guilty; here, I think I can say, even the guilty have no need to fear that they will get any worse punishment than they deserve.

Gentlemen, thank you again.

33. THE POLICE FORCE

Hints.—Usually this toast is proposed at a function of local interest, such as a municipal dinner. In such circumstances the speaker is usually a member of the municipal council who is not connected with the Police. The subject offers plenty of scope for humour, but this should not be overdone; it is important that a genuine tribute to the work of the Police should be included.

SPECIMEN

Gentlemen,—When American visitors come to this country and are asked for their impressions, many of them—especially the women—begin by saying, "I think your policemen are wonderful." For some peculiar reason this is generally regarded as a huge joke. Why it should be I cannot imagine; for I am not an American visitor, or even a woman, and I have never ceased to think that our policemen are wonderful.

Of course I must admit that I am prejudiced. Although I have lived a long life of crime, I have never been found out. Please don't think that this is because the police aren't up to their job; I am just the exception that proves the rule, and I hope that if I go on saying nice things about them, the police will allow me to remain exceptional.

So far I have had only one brush with the police, and that was not really a brush. It was over a little matter of parking on the wrong day or the wrong side, or probably both. I got off with a fatherly lecture and a promise to be a good boy in future.

Our Police are wonderfully fatherly, not only to the children who want to be helped across the road, but to men and women old enough to be their grandparents. Yet the thing that makes them so really wonderful is their good humour. You never see a bad-tempered policeman. You never find a policeman discourteous or even officious. Watch the way the Police handle a demonstration or a noisy crowd. They maintain order not by threats or blows, but by good humour and common sense. That is their peculiar genius.

Yet sometimes I wonder if we really appreciate what the Police do for us. I do not mean merely in its positive actions, but in its power to prevent crime. There are many views held these days on the value of punishment as a deterrent, and it is not my place to give a personal opinion on this subject. But I must express my absolute conviction that the greatest deterrent to crime is a strong and efficient Police. The criminal's concern about the punishment he will receive if he is caught is a secondary consideration; the thing that worries him most, and makes him think twice before committing a crime, is what the chances are of his being caught. Our greatest safeguard against crime is not the severity of the Law, but the figure of the policeman on the corner. And let us never forget that the policeman is always there; for whatever the provocation the Police never go on strike.

Gentlemen, I ask you to drink to the health of the Police Force, and I couple with this toast the name of Inspector ——.

USEFUL QUOTATIONS

When constabulary's duty to be done, a policeman's lot is not a happy one.—*Sir W. E. Gilbert.*

34. REPLY TO THE TOAST OF THE POLICE FORCE

SPECIMEN

Gentlemen,—I am happy to reply on behalf of the Police to the generous welcome you have given to this toast. Flattering things have been said about us, and I am almost tempted to say that I wouldn't have the heart to arrest the proposer of the toast even if I did catch him out. But you know that policemen have no hearts.

I am not going to indulge in false modesty and contradic' the compliments that have been paid to the Police Force, because I am proud enough to think that it compares pretty well with the Police in other countries. But the credit for this is not ours. It is yours. Nowhere in the world is there such a peaceful, law-abiding people as in Britain. A Police Force may be described as the discipline of the Law; and discipline has to be enforced only when self-discipline is absent. In this country self-discipline is a common possession.

You have spoken of the good-humoured way in which the Police deal with noisy crowds and demonstrations. The simple fact is that good humour is the only language a British crowd understands. The crowds themselves are so good-humoured that no other treatment is possible.

Finally, I should like to say that we regard ourselves not only as the custodians of the peace but also as the servants of the public. And it is a good public, and a good service to be in. Thank you, gentlemen.

35. THE FIRE BRIGADE

Hints.—See under The Police Force; but there should be rather less humour, and more stress laid on the heroic nature of the firemen's duties.

SPECIMEN

Gentlemen,—I am going to let you into a secret. When I was younger and wiser—and on both counts that means many years ago—I had one great ambition in life. That was that when I grow up I should become a fireman.

Well, I never achieved that ambition. That was my loss—

and, no doubt, the Fire Brigade's gain. But I never really succeeded in conquering the desire, and today, as in those early years, I am always thrilled and excited when I see a gleaming fire engine racing along the street with the bell clanging and the firemen tense and ready for action.

Fortunately I have never had to entertain the Fire Brigade at home in its official capacity. But I have seen it at work elsewhere, and have marvelled at the skill and courage of the men. And I have been over the scene of a fire after it has been put out by the Brigade, and I have marvelled again at the way in which property has been saved from damage. The Brigade's greatest work is the saving of life, and you know what heroism is shown for this purpose. But the Brigade also saves property, and the men who fight the fire show such wonderful skill and restraint—often at great personal danger—that much is preserved that would surely be lost under less careful hands.

We are lucky in this district. We have a Fire Brigade that can hardly have any equal in efficiency of organization and personal zeal. It is the best insurance policy we have, for it gives us a feeling of security that could not otherwise be obtained.

Gentlemen, I ask you to drink to the men of our Fire Brigade.

USEFUL QUOTATIONS

Fire—the most tangible of all visible mysteries.—*Leigh Hunt*.

Fire that's closest kept burns most of all.—*Shakespeare*.

Forewarned, forearmed; to be prepared is half the victory.—*Cervantes*.

Keep the home fires burning.—*Ivor Novello*.

36. REPLY TO THE TOAST OF THE FIRE BRIGADE

SPECIMEN

Gentlemen,—I am happy to reply to your kind toast to the Fire Brigade. We do not deserve the compliments you have paid us, for happily it is not very often that we have to fight a really big fire. You may be interested to hear a few statistics. In the last month we have answered fourteen calls. As a result of this activity we put out two small fires; observed the remains of two others that were privately extinguished before our arrival; observed vague evidence of two more that had not got the strength to keep burning for us; sought hard for three fires that were reported but never seem to have caught alight; and rescued five cats from uncomfortable positions that had nothing to do with fire at all.

Please do not think I am complaining about the shortage of fires. On the contrary, I want to thank you all for the care you show in preventing outbreaks. We should prefer you to train your cats to study their lines of retreat; but we would rather rescue your cats than have to break your windows and doors and ruin your personal possessions with water.

Gentlemen, on behalf of the Fire Brigade I thank you.

Chapter VII

THE CHURCH

37. THE BISHOP

Hints.—This toast is usually proposed by the chairman (a layman) at a mixed gathering of clergy and laity. The theme should be the hard work put in by the clergy in general and the Bishop in particular. Humour, unless very gentle, is not recommended for any but a practised speaker, and the speaker should be careful to avoid any controversial subject.

SPECIMEN

Gentlemen,—It is my honour and privilege to ask you to drink to the health of our Bishop. It would be impertinent of me to try to tell you of the great work he does in our Diocese, and in any case this would be impossible. You all know much of what the Bishop has done for us; but you know, too, that he does very much more which is concealed from public notice. Our Bishop does good with such stealth that he is rarely found out, even by accident. I have caught him out once or twice, but I am not going to give him away.

Tomorrow we shall have the pleasure of hearing the Bishop preach. Those who have heard him before know that this will be indeed a pleasure. But it is not merely as a great preacher that our Bishop demands our respect; it is, rather, by the example that he sets us. He does not only tell us how we can lead the Christian life; by his own life he shows us what a Christian is.

Gentlemen, I have great pleasure in proposing the health of our Bishop.

USEFUL QUOTATIONS

An honest man's the noblest work of God.—*Alexander Pope.*

God often visits us, but most of the while we are not at home.—*Roux*.

To yield reverence to another, to hold ourselves and our lives at his disposal, is the noblest state in which a man can live in this world.—*Ruskin*.

It is well said, in every sense, that a man's religion is the chief fact with regard to him.—*Thomas Carlyle*.

In religion, as in friendship, they who profess most are the least sincere.—*Sheridan*.

Religion is civilization, the highest.—*Disraeli*.

Whatever makes men good Christians makes them good citizens.—*Webster*.

He whose goodness is part of himself is what is called a real man.—*Mencius*.

I would rather have the affectionate regard of my fellow-men than I would have heaps and mines of gold.—*Dickens*.

38. THE CLERGY

Hints.—See under The Bishop.

SPECIMEN

Gentlemen,—It is my happy privilege to propose the health of our Bishop and clergy. Our debt to them is considerable. Not only are they our spiritual advisers and helpers, but they are also our friends. It is impossible to estimate how much good they have caused, and how much evil they have prevented, by their social work in our Diocese. They would not like to hear any estimate of this kind, even if it could be made; for individually and collectively, they prefer to hide their lights under bushels.

We are very happy to have the Bishop with us today. We do not see him very often, but we know that the Diocese is large and others need his presence more than we. But I must express our appreciation of the magnificent work he has done, which is the inspiration of all who try to lead a Christian life.

Gentlemen, I give the toast of the Bishop and his Clergy.

USEFUL QUOTATIONS

See under The Bishop.

39. THE VICAR

Hints.—*See under* The Bishop. Here, however, the speech should be less formal and more humorous, as the Vicar will probably be a friend of the speaker.

SPECIMEN

Gentlemen,—Popularity, like happiness, is elusive for those who seek it, and yet comes easily to those who never think about it. That is why our Vicar is such a popular man. I have never known him do or say a single thing for the sake of public favour. I have known him do and say several things that seemed likely to incur public disfavour. Yet the fact is that there is no one in this parish who is so well loved and respected as our Vicar. He is our guide, counsellor, and friend—a good companion on sunny days, and a sympathetic and wise adviser and helper when things go wrong.

Our Vicar is certainly not a worldly man, but he is a man of the world. I can think of no department in our parish life in which he does not play an active part. He is a star turn at our concerts. On the cricket field his leg-spinners have gained a reputation that I can only describe as unholy. His presence gives zest to every social function we have. I am told that no Women's Institute function would be worth holding without the Vicar, and I know that the ladies regard him as—well, gentlemen, there are too many husbands here for me to continue with this theme.

Nothing that I can say can do full justice to the Vicar, so I shall say no more, and just ask you to join me in drinking to his health. Gentlemen—the Vicar!

USEFUL QUOTATIONS

See under The Bishop.

40. THE CHURCHWARDENS

Hints.—This toast is usually proposed by one of the clergy, and its purpose is to give recognition to the work of the laity in helping the Church.

SPECIMEN

Gentlemen,—The work of the Church, like the game of cricket, is shared between amateurs and professionals, or Gentlemen and Players. Speaking as one of the least distinguished of the Players—a No. 11 batsman if ever there was one—I have the happy task of proposing the health of the Gentlemen, and in particular of those fine all-rounders, the Churchwardens.

My dictionary gives three definitions of a warden. The first describes him as a watchman or sentinel, but this definition is parenthetically—and, it seems to me, disparagingly—labelled "armchair". The second definition is that the warden is a guardian, president, or governor, as of a college. Finally my dictionary tells me, rather surprisingly, that a warden is a kind of cooking pear.

Now, gentlemen, the second definition is clearly inappropriate. Our churchwardens are not presidents or governors—although I have not the slightest doubt that they would make very good ones. Nor, I think, can they be fairly labelled as cooking pears. They are the wrong shape for that. So we must fall back on the first definition, which seems admirable except for the word "archaic". This is most unfair, for they are both energetic and active.

But they certainly are watchmen and sentinels. As the amateurs, or Gentlemen, in the team, they keep us professionals up to scratch. As good all-rounders, they take a big share in both the batting and bowling, and it is hard to imagine how we could manage without them.

Gentlemen, I ask you to give a hearty response to the toast of—the Churchwardens.

USEFUL QUOTATIONS

You can only make others better by being good yourself.—*Hawers.*

We can all be angry with our neighbour. What we want is to be shown, not his defects, of which we are too conscious, but his merits, to which we are too blind.—*R. L. Stevenson*.

There can hardly, I believe, be imagined a more desirable pleasure than that of praise unmixed with any possibility of flattery.—*Sir Richard Steele*.

See also under The Bishop.

41. REPLY TO THE TOAST OF THE CHURCHWARDENS

Hints.—This speech, made by one of the churchwardens, is largely governed by what was said by the proposer of the toast. Generally speaking, however, it will consist of a modest disavowal of the kind things said by the previous speaker, and an expression of pleasure in the duties of churchwarden. This speech needs humour.

SPECIMEN

Gentlemen,—Our Vicar has said some very kind things about us Churchwardens, and he has put me in a very difficult position. If I accept all these compliments without demur, I shall not only be lacking in modesty, but also guilty of suppressing the truth. If, on the other hand, I deny the justice of his remarks, I shall be suggesting that the Vicar himself has not been speaking the truth. Now you all know that the Vicar is the most honest of men, and that he is quite fearless in the matter of speaking the truth. You must therefore be puzzled to know how he can have come to say such nice things about men who have done nothing to deserve them. Fortunately there is an answer to the question, which both absolves the Vicar from the charge of dishonesty and yet puts us Churchwardens in their proper place.

The fact of the matter is simply that the Vicar has a happy habit of seeing the good in the worst of us. He showed this to me quite clearly the other day, when we made a train journey together. According to the time-table we should have arrived at our destination just in time for lunch; but in fact we still had a fair way to go when lunch-time arrived. I put this down to the inefficiency of the railway, but the Vicar's opinion was that he must have made a mistake in reading the time-table. That, by the way. The train stopped at a station, and we learned that it was unlikely to remain there for more than a minute or so. Rather regretfully we decided that there was no time even for a dash to the buffet to get something to eat. However, a rather grimy little boy was standing on the platform, and the Vicar beckoned to him.

"Here's a shilling," he said. "Now will you go to the buffet and buy three fourpenny buns, and bring back two for my friend and myself. The other one is for you."

The boy seized the shilling and dashed off to the buffet. I shook my head sadly.

"I don't think we'll see him again," I said. "Or your shilling."

The Vicar chided me gently for my lack of faith in human nature.

"He'll come back," he said confidently. And I knew it was useless to argue, because even if the boy didn't come back the Vicar would have found some excuse for him.

As it happened, however, the boy did return, with a bun wedged firmly in his mouth. But that was the only bun he had, and when he reached the window of our carriage he thrust eightpence into the Vicar's hand.

"Sorry," he said between mouthfuls. "They only had one left."

And then, gentlemen, the Vicar thanked him gravely and turned to me and said:

"You see? I told you he was an honest lad."

And that story, I think, explains why you have heard things said about the Churchwardens that must differ greatly from your own knowledge of us. Gentlemen, on behalf of my colleagues, I thank you.

HUMOROUS ANECDOTES

Many good stories are told about Vicars and Curates, and it is usually quite easy to work one into a speech connected with the Church. Here are a few examples:

The Vicar's son was a wild youth, and he returned like the prodigal on a cold winter's evening. His father happened to be entertaining two fellow ministers, and after eating a meal the young man found them in the lounge, standing in front of the fire and talking with their host. Introductions were made, but the boy was obviously in a sulky temper.

One of the guests, who had no idea of the real state of affairs, but was told merely that the Vicar's son had been away from home for a while, asked where he had been.

"In hell," said the boy bluntly.

There was a slight pause, and then the Vicar asked in a matter-of-fact voice:

"And what was it like there?"

"Much the same as here," was the reply. "Couldn't see the fire for parsons!"

The Vicar was the subject of a furious verbal onslaught by one of his parishioners. He made little reply to the attack, but allowed the man to continue his abuse. The parishioner, angered by the Vicar's refusal to argue, burst out as a parting shot:

"If I had an imbecile son, I would put him into the Church. What have you got to say to that?"

"Only that I am glad that your father did not share your view," was the mild reply.

Sunday School Teacher: "Can any boy tell me what children go to Heaven?"

Nasty Little Boy: "Dead 'uns."

The new Vicar officiated for the first time, and as the congregation left the church after the service, one of the members whispered to a sidesman:

"I have nothing but praise for our new Vicar."

"So I observed when I took the bag round," replied the sidesman drily.

The Vicar was trying to persuade the local spendthrift to make better provision for his wife and children.

"How much do you earn?" he asked.

"Seven pounds a week when the tax is off," was the reply.

"And you spend it all?"

"Certainly not," replied the spendthrift indignantly. "Never more than six pounds, sometimes less."

The Vicar was puzzled.

"Then surely you must have something saved," he said. "If you can put at least a pound a week aside——"

"Put it aside?" repeated the spendthrift in astonishment. "Of course I don't. I give it all to my wife—how else do you think she could run the house?"

CHAPTER VIII

THE SCHOOL

42. SPEECH DAY: PRESENTATION OF THE PRIZES

Hints.—The speaker must remember that a large part of his audience consists of boys or girls, and he should adapt his speech accordingly. But he should not "talk down"; and above all, he should not tell his audience that schooldays are "the happiest days of your life".

SPECIMEN

Ladies and Gentlemen,—A few moments ago, while I was sitting on this platform, feeling sorry for myself because I had got to make a speech, my thoughts went back to the last Speech Day I attended. It was, in fact, my last Speech Day at school. I remember it very well, because I happened to win a prize. The reason why I remember it is because it was the only prize I ever won all the time I was at school.

Now on that occasion a very distinguished gentleman came to the school to present the prizes. (Nowadays, of course, this job is done by very undistinguished people.) This gentleman followed the custom and made a speech, and I shall never forget what he said. You see, I was feeling rather pleased with myself, because I had won this prize and my parents were there to see me go up and collect it. And I thought the speaker was going to say what a fine thing it was to win a prize.

But he did not say that. He told us about his school-days, just as I am telling you about mine. And he told us that he had never won a prize. He went on to imply that he did not think much of those who did. Chaps who never won prizes, he said, nearly always made a tremendous success of life; while those who walked off with piles of books under their arms—well, he didn't actually *say* they all ended up in the gutter or in gaol, but that was the impression we got. And if I were to meet him again today, I suppose he would say that the only reason that I didn't end up in the gutter or gaol was that I only got one prize in the whole of my school career.

Now I am not going to make a speech like that. In fact, I am not going to make a speech at all. I am just going to present the prizes, and I want to say to the winners now that I offer them my hearty congratulations. I don't think any of them will end up in the gutter or gaol, and they have every right to be proud of their success. I will add that winning prizes at school does not mean that you are bound to make a success of life, any more than not winning prizes means that you are going to be a failure. We cannot all win prizes. But let us give credit to those who do.

(*Follow with the presentation of the prizes.*)

43. SPORTS DAY: PRESENTATION OF CUPS AND SPOONS

Hints.—See under Speech Day.

SPECIMEN

Ladies and Gentlemen,—Before I present the prizes, I am expected to make a speech. You probably think that is hard on you, but I assure you that it is much harder on me. So for my sake as well as yours, it is going to be short.

I have seen a magnificent display of athletics today. And when I say magnificent, I am not referring only to the time-keeper's records, although these reveal some pretty fine achievements. But the really fine thing was the spirit shown by the competitors—by all the competitors, and not only those who won prizes.

Now I do not want to belittle the victors. You have heard it said that we should count the game above the prize—and so we should; but that does not mean that the prize is of no value. Our first congratulations go to the winners, who have every right to be proud of their achievements. But we must also congratulate all the losers. Not because they lost—but because they did their best. They strove hard to win. They put out all their efforts; and what fine, courageous efforts they were!

So congratulations to you all—but especially to the winners.

(*Follow with the presentation of the prizes.*)

44. VOTE OF THANKS AFTER A SCHOOL CONCERT (OR PLAY)

Hints.—This speech is usually made by a parent. Follow the hints given under "Speech Day" and "Vote of Thanks to an Amateur Dramatic Society".

SPECIMEN

Ladies and Gentlemen,—A few days ago I was asked if I would propose a vote of thanks after the School Concert. That seemed to me almost as bad a task as having to get up on the stage and do a turn myself; so I sat down, and after a lot of labour I managed to write out a speech. Then I learned it by heart, and that was harder than learning Shakespeare. And now I cannot make the speech at all, because it would sound absurd after a Concert such as this. I expected it to be good, but I never thought it could be as good as it has been.

My own memory of school concerts is rather dim, but I know we never put on shows of this class. Acting, singing, dancing—everything has been really tip-top. You have given us a show that would shame most shows in the West End of London. I am not going to single out any particular item in the programme, because it was all good, and if I once started like that I should have to take up a lot of your time. But I must express my special appreciation of the way the staging and lighting were done. And so, to those who worked behind the scenes as well as those who entertained us from behind the footlights, I offer the appreciation and gratitude of the audience. Thank you all very much.

45. THE SCHOOL CHAPLAIN

Hints.—*See under* Speech Day *and* The Vicar.

SPECIMEN

Ladies and Gentlemen,—There are three good reasons
why my speech should be brief. One is that I don't like
speaking; another is, no doubt, that you don't like listening
to me. But the most important reason is that our Chaplain
is far too modest to enjoy hearing anyone sing his praises.
He has done so much for the School that it would be poor
return to embarrass him with an appreciation which could
not do him justice, anyway.

A School Chaplain, like an Army Padre, has to be a very
special sort of clergyman. All clergymen must know how to
preach; but the Chaplain and the Padre must know also
how not to preach. Our Chaplain has both qualifications,
and he uses them with excellent skill and proper timing. Not
only is he an inspiration to the whole School, but he is the
personal friend of every single boy.

Ladies and Gentlemen, I give you the toast of our
Chaplain.

USEFUL QUOTATIONS

See under The Bishop.

46. THE SCHOOL (AT AN OLD BOY'S DINNER)

Hints.—The toast is invariably proposed by an Old Boy,
and it should be quite brief and simple.

SPECIMEN

Gentlemen,—The Old School Tie has been the subject
of so many music-hall jokes that one might expect it to have
been laughed out of existence. Yet there seems to be plenty
of evidence to the contrary here tonight; and the fact that
it has survived so much ridicule surely proves that it is by
no means a meaningless symbol.

Most loyalties are difficult to explain, and loyalty to the
School is no exception. Old Boys' Associations differ from
most other societies in one important respect: their members

are not proposed and elected, and indeed have little say in
the matter of qualification for membership. The only thing
that we have in common, on the face of it, is that our respective parents happened to send us to the same educational
establishment; and one might ask what bond can exist among
us. The answer is not far to seek. As boys we were drawn
together in comradeship, not because we liked the look of
each other's faces—I am sure you will agree with me on
this point—but through loyalty to a common ideal.

The strength of that ideal lies in the fact, of which we
have abundant evidence here now, that it continues to hold
us together after the end of our communal life. It is not easy
to express its source of inspiration. It has nothing to do with
the School's scholastic or sporting achievements; it does not
derive from the School buildings or grounds; it does not
even come from the headmaster and the teaching staff—
saving their presence—although without their good influence
it could hardly survive. It is simply one of those imponder-
ables, and can only be defined as the Spirit of the School—
a spirit compounded of honour, teamwork, comradeship
and all that is best in communal life.

Gentlemen,—The School!

USEFUL QUOTATIONS

The future is purchased by the present.—*Dr. Johnson*.

A true and noble friendship shrinks not at the greatest
of trials.—*Jeremy Taylor*.

When men are friends, there is no need of justice;
but when they are just, they still need friendship.—*Aristotle*.

The belongings of friends are common.—*Aristotle*.

Sweet is the remembrance of troubles when you are in
safety.—*Euripides*.

Chapter IX

POLITICAL AND ELECTORAL

47. INTRODUCING THE CANDIDATE AT AN ELECTION MEETING

(Made by the Chairman)

Hints.—The difficulty in making a speech involving political considerations is not so much in the subject matter as in handling the audience. When you make a social speech or propose a convivial toast, you will find generally that your listeners will meet you in a friendly spirit; but whenever you have to touch on politics in public, you may be sure that at least a section of your audience will be hostile, and probably vocally so. Some general advice on dealing with hecklers has been given in Chapter III; and in preparing your speech you must keep this danger well in mind, and try to avoid including anything that will provoke awkward questions or facetious remarks intended to ridicule what you say.

In introducing a candidate you are not expected to go into details of his policy—that is the candidate's task. But your speech is important, because if it is properly prepared and delivered you can get the audience into the right spirit for listening to what the candidate has to say. Naturally your speech should be largely personal, but do not make the mistake of giving the candidate extravagant praise, which might provoke derision and therefore cause embarrassment.

SPECIMEN

Ladies and Gentlemen,—As chairman of this meeting I have the pleasure of introducing Mr. —— as candidate to represent the interests of this Borough in Parliament. As you know, he is the representative of the —— Party; and as you will have guessed, if you did not already know, I too am a supporter of that Party. I believe in its principles and its policy, and I am convinced that if it is returned to power at this Election—as I am sure it will be—every member of the community will benefit.

But I am not going to talk politics, or try to anticipate our candidate's speech. You have come to hear him, and I am not going to waste your time with a long introduction. All I want to say is that Mr. —— is, in my opinion, admirably fitted to represent this Borough, not only because his politics are sound—and they are very sound, as you will soon find out—but because he is a man of great personal integrity and ability. I commend him to you, ladies and gentlemen, and I trust you will give him the good hearing he deserves.

48. INTRODUCING THE CANDIDATE AT A MUNICIPAL ELECTION MEETING

(Made by the Chairman)

Hints.—*See under* Introducing the Candidate at an Election Meeting. Note also that this speech can be more personal and should include brief reference to topical local affairs. The subject matter of the speech will depend on whether the candidate represents the Party that had a majority before the Election or whether he belongs to the present Opposition. If for the former, the audience will need to be reminded of the work done; if the latter, the speech should be more critical of the present state of affairs. Again, however, the speaker should not try to anticipate what the candidate has to say.

SPECIMEN

Ladies and Gentlemen,—As chairman of this meeting I have the pleasure of introducing Mr.—— as a candidate for election to the Town Council. For good or bad, candidates for Municipal Elections, like General Elections, have to fight under Party labels. You know Mr. ——'s label, and you will have deduced that he has already been promised my support and my vote. But I ask you to regard him as something more than a good Party man. He has, I know, the very real interests of our town at heart, and he has both the energy and the ability to play an important part on our

Council. He is, of course, well known to many of you, and I am sure you could not find a man with a higher or saner sense of local patriotism.

I am not going to give you my own opinions on the present state of local politics, nor shall I pass any judgment on what has been done—or what has not been done—by the last Council. Each elector will make his own judgment on that when he records his vote. But I feel bound to remind you that there are a number of local problems that urgently need to be solved, and the next Council, however it is composed, will fail in its duty unless it tackles these with courage and resolution. There is, for example, the matter of (insert a reference to a topical local issue on which the candidate is taking a strong line). This problem is not new, and it must be apparent that it is unlikely to be solved unless we have a Council that is prepared to tackle it vigorously. Mr. —— has, I know, strong views on this and other pressing matters, which you are about to hear. I think he will satisfy you that his views are sound as well as strong; and I am convinced that he will make it quite clear that he has the energy and drive necessary to put them into practice. We need men of energy and drive on our Council.

Ladies and Gentlemen, your candidate—Mr. ——.

USEFUL QUOTATIONS

He served his party best, who serves the country best.—*Hayes*.

There is no perfecter endowment in man than political virtue.—*Plutarch*.

Can anybody remember when times were not hard and money not scarce?—*Emerson*.

We cannot eat the fruit while the tree is in blossom.—*Disraeli*.

Work is the great cure of all maladies and miseries that ever beset mankind.—*Carlyle*.

There's dignity in labour.—*Swain*.

49. PROPOSING THE ADOPTION OF A CANDIDATE FOR AN ELECTION

Hints.—Candidates for Elections are adopted at meetings

of the local Party, so here the issue is more personal than political. However, a candidate is adopted more for his political ability than for his personal qualities, and the speaker who proposes his adoption should base his case on this.

SPECIMEN

Mr. Chairman, Ladies and Gentlemen.—I have the agreeable task of proposing the adoption of Mr. —— as our candidate for the coming General Election. I am not going to support my proposal by drawing from my personal knowledge of Mr. ——, because the matter is too important for sentiment. We are all agreed that it is our task to choose the best possible candidate—that is, the candidate most likely to win the Election and to represent us in the way we would wish after he has been elected. I think that Mr. —— is entirely suitable on both counts. He has been very frank about his opinions on those points in the Party programme that concern us most, and I think you will agree that his views are entirely sound. He is a man of considerable political knowledge and experience, and he has that high degree of common sense necessary for a politician in dealing with those problems and issues that inevitably arise after the Election is over.

You all know that this is by no means an easy constituency, and only a strong candidate can have any hope of winning it. I think that Mr. —— has just the qualities that will appeal to the electorate. His public record is excellent, he has a most pleasant personality, he is an excellent speaker, and he impresses people as a man who will get things done. And I am sure that when he is elected he will get them done, too. It is therefore with every confidence that I propose that he should be formally adopted as our candidate.

50. OPPOSING THE ADOPTION OF A CANDIDATE FOR AN ELECTION

Hints.—This is not a particularly happy speech to have to make, but if it has to be made it needs to be expressed properly. Frankness is essential, of course; but it should not exceed the bounds of courtesy and decency. There must be no hint of personal abuse.

SPECIMEN

Mr. Chairman, Ladies and Gentlemen,—It is with very great regret that I have to oppose the recommendation to adopt Mr. —— as our candidate for the next Election. I must make it clear from the start that my opposition is in no way personal. I respect Mr. —— for his integrity and sincerity, and I am sure that if he were adopted he would not spare himself in trying to prove worthy of our trust; and that, if he were elected, he would make equally strenuous efforts to represent this constituency in a proper way.

But the matter is far too serious for good intentions to be accepted by themselves. Frankly, I do not think Mr. —— is suitable to represent either the Party or the constituency. He has been very frank in giving his opinions on various aspects of the Party programme, but on many points he does not appear to have understood all the implications. In particular, there is his attitude on the matter of. . . . His replies to various questions on this subject have been, to say the least, meagre and vague. I will not say they were deliberately evasive, because I am sure they were not; but I suggest to you that this is a question of vital importance to us as electors, and Mr. —— does not appear to have grasped its importance at all.

There are other matters on which Mr. ——'s views appear to be in conflict with our own. One is. . . . You will remember at previous meetings we have passed resolutions strongly in favour of. . . . The last occasion when we expressed this opinion was only three months ago. Mr.——, however, seems inclined to take a different view. Another point on which we are agreed is the matter of. . . . On this Mr. —— does not seem to have taken up a very definite position, but the little he has said does not appear to me to be in agreement with our own opinions.

What concerns me especially is that these issues, which Mr. —— treats rather casually, are bound to be raised by the other side in the coming Election campaign. They need to be faced by someone who understands the problems and appreciates our conception of how they can be solved. I am well aware that from a national point of view the Election will be fought on much broader lines; but you know that the people of this constituency are keenly interested in our local problems, and I am convinced that on the way these are handled by our candidate will depend the fate of many votes, if not the actual result of the poll.

I have no doubt that Mr. —— is a loyal member of the Party, and that he has the general ability to make an excellent Member of Parliament. But I do not think this is the right constituency for him. I am not making this criticism merely because he is not a local man; but I think he is unsuitable because he neither understands nor appreciates the importance of issues peculiar to this constituency, which will be widely discussed during the Election, and which will need to be brought to the attention of the Government— whatever the Government is—when the Election is over.

For these reasons I feel bound to oppose the adoption of Mr. —— as your candidate.

USEFUL QUOTATIONS

Better not do the deed than weep it done.—*Prior*.
Good rarely came from good advice.—*Lord Byron*.
Advice is seldom welcome, and those who want it the most always like it the least.—*Lord Chesterfield*.

51. OUR MEMBER OF PARLIAMENT

Hints.—The toast to the local M.P. may be proposed at a purely Party gathering or at a function where the audience is more general. In the latter case the speaker should steer clear of political controversy, for the proposal of a toast should be so worded that the toast itself will be readily acceptable by the whole audience.

SPECIMEN

Ladies and Gentlemen,—It is with great pleasure that I rise to propose the toast of our Member of Parliament. This is not a political function, and I am not going to make a political speech. Indeed, I am not going to make a speech at all, for I am sure that after the last stormy session at Westminster, Mr. —— has heard enough speeches to last him until the end of the recess. All I want to say is this.

Whatever our Member has said in the House of Commons —and he may be surprised to know how closely we read his speeches—he has never forgotten the interests of his constituents. On several occasions he has spoken up on our behalf, even at the risk of making himself unpopular with the Party to which he belongs; and ever since he was elected he has, I know, personally investigated every request and complaint that he has received from a constituent. His presence with us today is one more example of his concern with local affairs; and when he next presents himself to the electorate, whether we put him in again or cast him into the political wilderness, he may rest assured that the efforts he has made on our behalf as a community will have been both recognized and appreciated.

Ladies and Gentlemen, I give you the toast of Mr. ——, our M.P.

USEFUL QUOTATIONS

See under previous speeches in this chapter.

CHAPTER X

SOCIAL TOASTS

52. THE LADIES

Hints.—This toast is usually proposed by the youngest bachelor in the company, and the spirit of this choice should be reflected in his speech. It should be light-hearted but, of course, flattering to the fair sex. Humour is naturally desirable, but the speaker should exercise particular care to ensure that his jokes are in good taste. If a joke seems only a shade doubtful, it is better left out.

SPECIMEN

Gentlemen.—The task of proposing this toast has been given to me because I happen to be the youngest bachelor here tonight. I do not know the origin of this custom, but I imagine it must be because the youngest is the least likely to be a confirmed bachelor, and his single state is probably not due to any lack of appreciation of the opposite sex. In my own case I may as well admit that I am full of appreciation. The ladies here tonight have only a poor speaker to extol their charms, but they could not find a more devoted admirer.

I hope you will not think that because I am single, I know nothing about the ladies. I have not, of course, the same concentrated experience of a married man, but no doubt that will come later. Meanwhile I am steadily enlarging my knowledge of the fair sex in general—at least, to the extent that they will allow me. And every enlargement of my knowledge adds further to my admiration. The fact is, gentlemen, that the time seems to be approaching when I shan't be able to keep away from them!

We sometimes hear talk, even in these modern times, of the so-called equality of women, as though it were something to be argued about. I am neither a social historian nor a prophet, but I venture to suggest that such a thing as equality between the sexes has never existed and never will exist. Women have never been our equals; they have always been vastly superior to us. There would be more sense in talking about equality for men, but personally I hope it never comes to that. Let the ladies remain as different, as feminine, and as irresistible as they are now.

I ask you to join me in drinking to the health of all our charmers. Gentlemen—the Ladies!

USEFUL QUOTATIONS

Nature intended that woman should be her masterpiece. —*Lessing*.

O woman, lovely woman, nature made thee
To temper man; we had been brutes without you.
                              —*Thomas Otway*.

I for one venerate a petticoat.—*Lord Byron*.

The most beautiful object in the world, it will be allowed, is a beautiful woman.—*Lord Macaulay*.

Man has his will; but woman has her way.—*O. W. Holmes*.

53. REPLY TO THE TOAST OF THE LADIES

SPECIMEN

Gentlemen,—My difficulty in reply to your most generous toast is that I am not allowed to say what I want to. You are allowed to flatter us as much as you like—and almost as much as we like, but the only times when we are allowed to tell you what we think of you are when our thoughts are unfriendly. The primmest Victorian miss always had the right to say to a man, "Sir, your attentions are unwelcome; pray desist"; but today even, for all our much-vaunted freedom, no girl would dare to say to a man, "Sir, your attentions are very welcome; please carry on." That would be regarded as immodest, if not worse. All women are expected to have a natural modesty; but I suspect that the Frenchman Balzac got nearer the truth when he said that "woman's modesty is man's greatest invention."

So here I am, allowed to say no more than thank you

to the very kind compliments you have paid us. I dare not tell you in reply that I have been an admirer of men almost from the cradle; that I find you good to look at, pleasant to listen to, delightful to dance with, charming companions; that, in fact, I think you are wonderful! These are the things I dare not say—but perhaps now you will be able to guess them.

USEFUL QUOTATIONS

Woman will be the last thing civilized by man.—*George Meredith*.

A woman is only a woman, but a good cigar is a smoke.—*Rudyard Kipling*.

54. OUR GUESTS

Hints.—The specimen given below will need to be adapted to the nature of the function and especially to the guests who have been invited to attend. The proposer should include in his speech some complimentary allusions to the more prominent guests—including, of course, the guest who has been chosen to reply to the toast.

SPECIMEN

Ladies and Gentlemen,—It is my privilege to propose the health of our guests. It is an easy task, and requires few words and no formality from me; for most of our guests are not strangers. I hope that by the time they leave they will all think of themselves as our friends.

Some of our guests have travelled quite a long way to be with us tonight, and I know I am expressing the general opinion when I say how much we appreciate the compliment they have paid us in spending the evening with us. I only hope that they will not regret their kindness. I am reminded that the late George Bernard Shaw was once a guest at a social function and was asked afterwards what the company was like. "Terrible," he replied. "I should have been bored stiff if I hadn't been there." I hope none of our guests will think this worth quoting when they are asked the same question.

We are pleased to see with us (insert the allusions to prominent guests).

Finally, I want to say how much pleasure the presence of all our guests has given to us, and to express the hope that we shall have many opportunities of seeing more of them in the future and getting to know them better.

Gentlemen, I give you the toast of—our guests!

55. REPLY TO THE TOAST OF OUR GUESTS

SPECIMEN

Gentlemen,—When a man has been wined and dined in this regal fashion, his only concern is whether he can manage to get up on his feet and stay there long enough to express his thanks. I have, as you see, achieved the first part of this task; and the length of my speech will depend on how far I can carry out the second part. I can safely promise you that my subsidence will not be delayed for very long.

To thank you for your magnificent hospitality would be hard enough by itself, but you have made my task even harder. You have actually thanked us for coming here and enjoying that hospitality. You have even gone so far as to drink to our health, after you have done everything you could to undermine it. I can think of only one reply to your generous toast. Whatever difficulties we are going to have in getting home, we had none in getting here. There was absolutely no inconvenience to any of us. If we really earned your thanks by coming here—and it seems very difficult to believe—then we are ready to confer the same favour again as many times as you like!

Gentlemen, on behalf of the guests I offer you my warmest thanks for this most enjoyable evening.

56. ABSENT FRIENDS

Hints.—The speech should be short and sincere. Humour is best avoided, as flippancy is in bad taste. The specimen below needs to be adopted to suit the circumstances.

SPECIMEN

Ladies and Gentlemen,—You do not want a long speech to introduce this toast. It is a simple toast, with a wealth of meaning. Most of us have family and friends a long way away, whom we wish were with us now. Their presence would add to the enjoyment of our festivities. But I am sure that they would want us to enjoy ourselves just as much in their absence, and would ask no more than that we should make a brief pause to think of them for a few moments, and drink in silence to—Absent Friends.

USEFUL QUOTATIONS

Absent in body, but present in spirit.—*I Corinthians*.

57. THE BRIDE AND BRIDEGROOM

Hints.—This toast, which is usually proposed by an old friend of the bride, should be brief and tactful. The proposer should remember that the bride and groom are probably embarrassed, and he should not try to get cheap laughs at their expense.

SPECIMEN

Ladies and Gentlemen,—I have a happy duty to perform on this happy occasion. I am going to ask you all to drink to the health and happiness of the bride and groom. It is an especially happy task because I can perform it with such confidence. Both of them look the picture of health, and their happiness is beyond concealment.

Marriage has sometimes been called a lottery, but I am sure there is no gamble about this match. Both the bride and groom took a peek in advance at the winning numbers before they chose their tickets. Of course I could have told the groom that he had found a winner right from the start, for I have known the bride since she was a sweet and lovable child, and watched her become sweeter and more lovable as she grew up. But the groom wisely did not ask my opinion, and nor did the bride. I hope they will forgive me if I give it now, and say that if ever a marriage was made in heaven, this is it.

No one ever forgets his wedding day, and the young couple will look back on this day with sweet memories as the years pass. I doubt if their memories will include my speech, so I shall detain you no further. Ladies and Gentlemen, I ask you to drink to the health and happiness of the bride and groom.

USEFUL QUOTATIONS

Thy wife is a constellation of virtues; she's the moon, and thou art the man in the moon.—*Congreve.*

Of all actions of a man's life, his marriage does least concern other people; yet of all actions of our life 'tis most meddled with by other people.—*Table Talk.*

No woman should marry a teetotaller, or a man who does not smoke.—*R. L. Stevenson.*

58. REPLY TO THE TOAST OF THE BRIDE AND BRIDEGROOM

Hints.—This speech, which is always made by the bridegroom, can be very brief. No one expects a flow of oratory from a man who has just got married, and it is enough if he simply voices his thanks. Should he want to make a longer speech, he will naturally say how fortunate he considers himself, but he should not give a long list of the bride's qualities; nor should he forget to mention his appreciation of the kindness shown to him by her parents. It is usual for the bridegroom's speech to end with the toast of the bridesmaids.

SPECIMEN

Ladies and Gentlemen,—My wife and I—I must get used to this way of speaking—thank you all most sincerely for your kind wishes. I am sure you will excuse me from making a long speech, and will understand that at the moment I am quite incapable of making one. I don't need to tell you that I think I am the luckiest man in the world, and that my only ambition is to be worthy of my luck. I must add that today I have not only gained the best wife any man could have, but I have also acquired an extra mother and father. No parents could have been kinder to a man bent on stealing their daughter.

Before I sit down, I must ask you to join me in drinking to the health of the very charming ladies who have supported my wife in her ordeal—if that is the right word. Ladies and Gentlemen—to the Bridesmaids!

USEFUL QUOTATIONS

The most precious possession that ever comes to a man in this world is a woman's heart.—*Holland.*

59. THE BRIDESMAIDS

Hints.—Usually the proposal of this toast is included in the bridegroom's reply to the toast of the bride and bridegroom (see above). If it is a separate toast the speech is not easy to make, for the proposer's scope is limited; and, of course, he must take great care not to be tactless.

SPECIMEN

Ladies and Gentlemen,—I hope that the only two really important persons here will not mind if I distract your thoughts from them for a moment. Possibly they will even welcome a brief escape from the limelight; and I am sure they will agree that the subjects of my toast are well worth your attention. I mean, of course, the bridesmaids. The bride has told me that they have given her no end of help, and my own eyes tell me that their decorative value has greatly helped the success of the day. They have performed their duties so charmingly that I might be tempted to say that they should always be bridesmaids—but they are far too charming to have much chance of that!

Ladies and Gentlemen,—To the bridesmaids!

USEFUL QUOTATIONS

I have always thought that every woman should marry, and no man.—*Disraeli.*

See also *under* The Ladies.

60. REPLY TO THE TOAST OF THE BRIDESMAIDS

Hints.—This speech is invariably made by the best man, and again tact is essential.

SPECIMEN

Ladies and Gentlemen,—I am sure that the bridesmaids are very grateful for the kind things you have said about them. I cannot take it upon myself to voice their thoughts, because I am quite sure they are not the same as my own. When I am not thinking about the beautiful bride—and it is difficult to stop thinking about her—I find that my thoughts go automatically to the beautiful bridesmaids. As a matter of fact, although I do not know much about the origin of marriage customs, I suspect that one of their duties is to distract the best man's attention from the bride. For while my admiration for the bride must be tempered by proper respect for the groom, there is no such restraint on my feelings towards the bridesmaids; and—well, I think I had better stop before I give away too much, for I am still a bachelor.

61. THE BABY (AT A CHRISTENING PARTY)

Hints.—This toast is invariably proposed by the baby's godfather. It should be light-hearted and cheerful in character, and include a compliment to the mother and father. If the godfather is a grandfather, he can recall an anecdote about the mother or father as a baby.

SPECIMEN

Ladies and Gentlemen,—I have the greatest pleasure in proposing the health of our robust-looking guest of honour. This is his first real public appearance, and I am sure you will agree that he has made a big success of it. It is perhaps a little too early to discuss his character, but certainly he has already won all our hearts. Of course he ought to be a fine baby, because he has the finest start in life any baby can have: good parents. We know that they will give him all the love and care needed to make his childhood happy; and I am sure that he, in his turn, will give great joy to them. So I ask you to drink to the health of A—— B—— (the baby's names), and may he have a long and happy life.

USEFUL QUOTATIONS

Every baby born into the world is a finer one than the last.—*Charles Dickens.*

Children are the last word of human imperfection. They cry, my dear; they put vexatious questions; they demand to be fed, to be washed, to be educated, to have their noses blowed; and when the time comes, they break our hearts, as I break this piece of sugar.—*R. L. Stevenson.*

In general those parents have the most reverence who most deserve it.—*Dr. Johnson.*

62. REPLY TO THE TOAST OF THE BABY

(Made by the father)

SPECIMEN

Ladies and Gentlemen,—I must apologize on behalf of my son, who regrets that he is unable to reply to your kind toast himself, and has asked me to do the job for him. This is not the worst job I have had to do for him in his short life, and I do not doubt that harder tasks lie in store.

My wife and I are grateful to you for the very kind and flattering things you have said about us, which we do not deserve. We are very ordinary parents—but I hope you will pardon me if I point out that our child is no ordinary baby.

We want to thank you all for coming to give A—— (name of baby) your support on this important occasion of his life, and our special thanks are due to those who have kindly acted as his sponsors. May I ask you to drink their health too? Ladies and gentlemen, to the baby's godmother and godfathers!

63. A BIRTHDAY TOAST

Hints.—The character of the speech will naturally depend greatly on the age of the person whose birthday is being celebrated. The toast is usually proposed by an old friend, and he is allowed to relate some humorous anecdotes drawn from the friendship. While the proposer will naturally point out some of the good qualities of his friend, he should avoid fulsome praise or he will cause embarrassment and may appear insincere.

SPECIMEN

Ladies and Gentlemen,—I have been asked to propose this toast because I am A—— B——'s oldest friend. I am not sure if this does him justice. An old saying tells us that a man should be judged by his choice of friends, and I should hate to think that A——'s reputation was linked too closely to mine. I think I can say that it is only in this matter of choosing friends that I have better taste than he has.

But it is not merely for his good taste that A—— deserves our good wishes. I am not going to embarrass him by reciting a catalogue of his many fine qualities, but I think he will forgive me if I tell you of just one little experience that we shared many years ago. (Describe an incident to the credit of the subject of the toast.)

So, ladies and gentlemen, I ask you to join me in drinking the health of A—— B—— and in wishing him many happy returns of his birthday. May he have many more birthdays to come!

USEFUL QUOTATIONS

A faithful friend is the medicine of life.—*Apochrypha.*

They are rich who have true friends.—*Thomas Fuller.*

The ornament of a house is the friends who frequent it. —*Emerson.*

A friend may well be reckoned the masterpiece of nature. —*Emerson.*

If he have not a friend, he may quit the stage.—*Francis Bacon.*

Be slow in choosing a friend, slower in changing.—*Benjamin Franklin.*

The highest friendship must always lead us to the highest pleasure.—*Henry Fielding.*

Friendship is the gift of the gods, and the most precious boon to man.—*Benjamin Disraeli.*

64. REPLY TO A BIRTHDAY TOAST

Hints.—Express surprise about all the good things said of you, and do not add to them. Be brief.

SPECIMEN

Ladies and Gentlemen,—C—— D—— (name of proposer) has done me many acts of friendship in the past, and I have always appreciated them; but today, I think, he has been much too kind and not very truthful. He has credited me with virtues I have never possessed, and conveniently forgotten all my many failings. I am not going to correct him, because if I did you would start doubting whether any friend of mine could be as fine a man as you know C—— to be. The fact is that I am lucky in my friends, and the proof of my good fortune is in the company that has honoured me by coming here today. There is an old saying, "Be sure your friends will find you out." I don't believe it, for my friends have never found me out, and I hope they never do. Ladies and gentlemen, thank you very much for your kind wishes.

65. AT A COMING OF AGE (OF A MAN)

Hints.—See under A Birthday Toast.

SPECIMEN

Ladies and Gentlemen—It is my very pleasant duty to propose the heath of A—— B—— on reaching his majority. I will not use the expression "coming of age," for frankly, I dislike it. If age comes at twenty-one, then I must have died years ago. And how can you think of age when you look at our young friend? To me he represents the coming of youth. He is old only in the sense that he has now reached the age when most people stop wanting to be older. Happily he has a good many years to enjoy before he will reach the age when he will start to want to be younger.

Some people never grow up, and others are old for their age; I hope A—— will take it as a compliment when I express the opinion that he seems to me to be absolutely twenty-one in every respect. I am not going to embarrass him by reciting a catalogue of his many fine qualities, nor am I going to bore him with the advice of an older man, which he would probably ignore anyway. I think it was Somerset Maugham who said that there is a sort of conspiracy among older folks to pretend that they are wiser than younger folks, and the younger folks do not rumble it until they themselves have got older—and then, of course, it pays them to join in the conspiracy, so that it goes on for ever.

I am sure that A—— B—— will live a happy, successful and useful life, for he has all the qualities necessary for this enviable trinity. So, ladies and gentlemen, I give you this toast. To our good friend A—— B——.

"For he's a jolly good fellow, etc."

66. ALTERNATIVE SPECIMEN

(Suitable when the proposer is an older man and an intimate friend of the family)

Ladies and Gentlemen.—No one could have more pleasure than I in proposing the health of A—— B—— on this important occasion. I have known him for a long time—longer, indeed than he has known me; for when I first set eyes on him he was an infant in his nurse's arms. I shall not embarrass him by recalling my memories of the first of his seven ages, although it is only fair to say that I have no recollection of him either mewling or puking. Nor, as a schoolboy, did he ever whine. Whether or not he had a shine on his morning face is outside my knowledge, but I know he was boyish enough to creep, if not like a snail, at least pretty unwillingly to school.

The first two of his seven ages are past now, and according to Shakespeare we shall next see him as a lover—

> "Sighing like a furnace, with a woeful ballad
> Made to his mistress' eyebrow."

It is not an easy picture to imagine. I have rarely heard A—— sigh, and never like a furnace. If he has poetic talent he has kept it well hidden, and I am sure his ballads would be anything but woeful. And in any case, ladies' eyebrows are not what they were in Shakespeare's day. But I have no doubt that A—— will make—if he has not already made—speedy conquests of the hearts of the ladies, for his good qualities are quite exceptional. And I have less doubt that his life will continue to be happy, successful, and useful. So I ask you to drink to the health of A—— B——.
"For he's a jolly good fellow, etc."

USEFUL QUOTATIONS

The youth of a nation are the trustees of posterity.—*Benjamin Disraeli*.

They can conquer who believe they can.—*Emerson*.

A wise man makes more opportunities than he finds.—*Francis Bacon*.

If youth be a defect, it is one that we outgrow only too soon.—*J. R. Lovell*.

Those who make the worst use of their time most complain of its shortness.—*La Bruyère*.

67. REPLY TO A COMING OF AGE TOAST (BY A MAN)

Hints.—See under Reply to a Birthday Toast.

SPECIMEN

Ladies and Gentlemen,—I have heard it said that young men think older men are fools, and that older men *know* young men to be so. One day I shall learn how far true the second part of the saying is; I hope it is not entirely accurate, for I can say quite honestly that I do not hold with the first part. For the moment I must express my thanks for the honour you have paid me on this rather important occasion to myself. I must also thank you very much for not asking me how it feels to be twenty-one, for of course it feels just the same as twenty.

I am not going to attempt to reply to the compliments you have paid me, which are entirely undeserved; but I feel bound to say one thing. Whatever advantages I have in life I owe entirely to my mother and father. If I succeed in anything, it is thanks largely to them; if I fail, the fault lies with myself. If I can live up to their standards I shall think myself a lucky man. Once again, thank you very much.

68. AT A COMING OF AGE (OF A WOMAN)

Hints.—See under A Birthday Toast.

SPECIMEN

Ladies and Gentlemen,—My task tonight is an honour rather than a duty, for I am sure that I am generally envied for being chosen to propose the health of A—— B—— on her twenty-first birthday. My only qualification is that I have had the privilege of wishing her many happy returns on most of her other birthdays. I can even remember her first birthday, when I took her in my arms, and later occasions when she sat on my knee. You will, I am sure, appreciate that I recall these things rather wistfully, for I am unlikely to get any further opportunities of this nature.

I have watched A—— grow up. I have seen childish prettiness give way to womanly beauty; I have seen good nature broaden into charm. To me she has always been sweet and lovable, and I am sure she will remain the same for the rest of her life. Ladies and Gentlemen, I ask you to join me in drinking the health of A—— B—— and wishing her many happy returns of her twenty-first birthday.

USEFUL QUOTATIONS

See under At a Coming of Age (of a man) *and* The Ladies.

69. REPLY TO A COMING OF AGE TOAST (BY A WOMAN)

Hints.—No formal speech is required or even desirable. All that the lady is expected to do is to get up and voice her thanks in her own words.

SPECIMEN

Ladies and Gentlemen.—Please don't ask me for a speech. You have made me all bubbling over inside, and I don't know how to say all I think. Just one thing I can say, and mean it with all my heart: thank you, thank you—thank you!

70. AT A SILVER WEDDING PARTY

Hints.—The speech, which is usually made by the oldest friend of the married couple, should be quiet and sincere.

SPECIMEN

Ladies and Gentlemen,—I can almost say that I have looked forward to this moment for twenty-five years, for I was present at the wedding of the charming couple in whose honour I am speaking tonight. It is sometimes said that a friend who marries is a friend lost; but when A—— B—— got married, I not only retained his friendship, but gained another friend too. For twenty-five years I have enjoyed the kindness of our host and hostess, and if I can enjoy the same friendship until their wedding turns from silver to gold, then I shall be very happy.

It is, I think, just as well that I am here tonight to vouch for the authenticity of the celebration. Had I not had the proof of my own eyes, I should find it hard to believe that our host and hostess have been married so long. In looks and spirit they are both so much younger than their years; and their obvious delight in each other could not be surpassed by newly weds. I think I can say that their honeymoon has lasted for twenty-five years, and looks like lasting for the rest of their lives.

Let us drink to their health, and wish them as much happiness together in the future as they have had in the past. They could not have more. Ladies and gentlemen, to Mr. and Mrs. B——.

USEFUL QUOTATIONS

No woman should marry a teetotaller, or a man who does not smoke.—*R. L. Stevenson.*

Well-married, a man is winged; ill-matched, he is shackled.—*Beecher.*

See also under The Bride and Bridegroom.

71. REPLY TO A SILVER WEDDING TOAST

(By the husband)

SPECIMEN

Ladies and Gentlemen,—I have been looking forward to this opportunity of expressing the thanks of my wife and myself for your kind wishes and many charming gifts to mark this occasion in our married life. Now you have placed us further in your debt by your most generous response to this toast, and made my task more difficult than ever. Indeed, I can recall only one other occasion in my life when I had to get up and try to express feelings that could not be done full justice by any words. That occasion, of course, was exactly twenty-five years ago today. All I could manage to stammer out then was that I thought I was the luckiest man in the world; and all I can stammer out now is that I know I am the luckiest man in the world.

For twenty-five years I have enjoyed life with the perfect wife, while she has suffered a husband imperfect in all save one thing: his love for her. We have been happy together, and I think we should have been happy on a desert island; but we have not lived apart from the world, and a good deal of our mutual happiness has been brought to us by common friends. Tonight those friends are with us. And so we thank you all, not only for your kind wishes and presents, but for the joys you have given us since we were married.

USEFUL QUOTATIONS

Every woman should marry—and no man.—*Benjamin Disraeli*.

Is not marriage an open question, when it is alleged, from the beginning of the world, that such as are in the institution wish to get out, and such as are out wish to get in?—*Emerson*.

Advice to persons about to marry: Don't.—*Punch's Almanack*.

Strange to say what delight we married people have to see these poor fools decoyed into our condition.—*Samuel Pepys*.

72. THE SPIRIT OF CHRISTMAS

Hints.—Speeches are not usual at a family Christmas party, but where the gathering includes friends as well as relatives, a formal proposal of this toast may be desired. The note should, of course, be of cheer and conviviality.

SPECIMEN

Ladies and Gentlemen,—Christmas, as you all know, is the festival for young children. It is for their sake that we decorate our homes with holly and mistletoe. It is for their sake that we put on paper hats and play jolly games. It is for their sake that we eat turkey and Christmas pudding and a whole variety of other good things. It is for their sake alone—or so we say; and if you believe that, you can believe it is for the sake of the children, too, that we drink port and smoke cigars on this occasion.

Please do not think I am decrying the idea that Christmas is primarily a children's feast-day. On the contrary, its great merit is that it makes children of us all. It is the one time in the year when we can forget our grown-up dignity and have a good time. This, I think is the spirit of Christmas, and I ask you to join me in drinking to it.

USEFUL QUOTATIONS

When the turkey's on the table and the candles on the tree, I'm jest about as happy as I ever wanta be.

My children gathered round me an' my neighbours settin'
    by,
I couldn't be no happier, an' I don't wanta try.
Carolyn Wells.

Christmas comes! He comes, he comes,
  Hollies in the window greet him,
  Gifts precede him, bells proclaim him,
  Every mouth delights to name him.
—*Leigh Hunt.*

73. HAPPY NEW YEAR

Hints.—The passing of the old year and the coming in of
the new may be celebrated with a toast preceded by a brief
speech of proposal. The chief point to emphasize is success
to those present and to absent friends. Timing is important.

SPECIMEN

Ladies and Gentlemen,—There is no danger of my de-
taining you for long, for it is almost midnight. When the
clock strikes, and the bells ring, I am going to ask you to drink
with me to a happy and successful New Year, and to our
reunion here in exactly a year's time. As we drink the toast
I ask you to spare a thought for absent friends, and let us
hope that next year they will be with us. Ladies and gentlemen—the hour is striking—I give you the toast of a Happy
New Year!

74. A SMOKING CONCERT (OPENING REMARKS)

Hints.—These remarks are made by the chairman, and
they should be as brief as possible. All that the speaker has
to do is to start the ball rolling, welcome any distinguished
entertainers, and remind the audience of details of procedure.

SPECIMEN

Gentlemen,—We are here tonight to be entertained, and
I happen to know that there is plenty of excellent entertain-

ment in store. My remarks do not come under this heading, but you will be happy to learn that I have already nearly finished my speech. All that remains for me to say is that we are very pleased to welcome Mr.—— and Mr. ——, who have kindly come along to amuse us in their own inimitable way. Our other entertainers you already know, and their names are a guarantee of the good things in store. Finally, may I remind you—without offence, I hope—of our custom of ordering refreshments between items only.

There it is, gentlemen; and now I call upon Mr. —— to open our programme.

75. A SMOKING CONCERT (CLOSING REMARKS)

Hints.—These remarks also are made by the chairman, and should be equally brief.

SPECIMEN

Gentlemen,—Before we break up this delightful gathering, you will, I am sure, want me to express your gratitude to those who have made the evening such a great success. I do not need to comment on the entertainment, because you have already shown your appreciation with noisy enthusiasm; I only want to ask you to be noisy just once more in honour of all the entertainers.

Chapter XI

SPORTING TOASTS

76. OUR OPPONENTS (CRICKET)

Hints.—Of course sportsmanship is the keynote of this toast, with emphasis on friendly rivalry and the fact that the game is more important than the result. If your own side has won, make little of the success, mention any luck you may have had, and dwell on the difficulty your team experienced before it could claim the victory. If your side has lost, do not bemoan the absence of your best players or claim that you were unlucky; say that the better team won, and that you hope to get your revenge next time.

Often the convention is for the toast to be proposed by the captain of the winning team and answered by his opposite number; but sometimes the toast is proposed by the captain of the home team, irrespective of the result of the match.

SPECIMEN

Gentlemen,—I have the greatest pleasure in proposing to you the toast of our opponents. I know you will agree with me that we had an excellent game. As it happened, we managed to scrape a win, and on paper it may look a comfortable victory. In fact, as you all know, our opponents gave us some very uncomfortable moments, and the score-book flatters us. Of course I am glad we won; but I am still gladder that we had such a good game. Our opponents were not only keen and able players—their fielding, in particular, was a lesson to us—but they showed themselves fine sportsmen. It is not for the result that we shall remember this game so much as the spirit in which it was played. The next time we meet we shall try to win again—although I don't mind admitting that we expect at least as hard a struggle as we had today, but whatever the result, we know in advance that we shall have a good game, played in the spirit in which cricket should always be played.

Gentlemen, I give you the toast of our opponents, the
——— (name of club), coupled with the name of their captain,
A—— B——.

USEFUL QUOTATIONS

Always play fair, and think fair; and if you win don't
crow about it; and if you lose don't fret.—*Eden Phillpotts*.

Success is sweet: the sweeter if long delayed and attained
through manifold struggles and defeats.—*Leigh Hunt*,
"Table Talk".

77. REPLY TO THE TOAST OF OUR OPPONENTS (CRICKET)

Hints.—See under Our Opponents (Cricket).

SPECIMEN

Gentlemen,—On behalf of a very chastened team, I wish
to thank you for your most cordial toast. We have been
soundly beaten, and I had no intention to try to make
excuses; but I did not expect to hear excuses made for us.
You are too generous in your victory, and I can only reply
by saying that the better team won, and we know it. But it is
a great comfort to hear that you do not consider your afternoon was entirely wasted, or that you might have done better
at the nets. Whatever faults there were in our play—and I
know there were plenty—we tried our hardest to give you a
good game. The simple fact was that you were too good for
us. But we enjoyed the match tremendously, and it is a relief
to hear that you got some pleasure out of it.

I must thank you also for the way you have entertained us.
providing us with a magnificent tea (and dinner) which we
did little to deserve.

According to my memory, a fixture has been arranged
for a return match in six weeks' time. Then we shall have
the pleasure of offering you our hospitality—which I am
afraid will hardly equal yours—and, we hope, of avenging
today's defeat. It may seem boastful to make this suggestion,
after our performance today; but like most cricketers, we

never know when we are beaten, and the next time we take the field against you we shall be more determined than ever. Anyway, whatever the result, I share your knowledge that we are going to have another good, sporting game.

On behalf of the —— (name of club), gentlemen, I thank you.

78. OUR OPPONENTS (ASSOCIATION FOOTBALL)

Hints.—See under Our Opponents (Cricket). Both these toasts can be easily adapted for other team sports.

SPECIMEN

Gentlemen,—I have great pleasure in asking you to drink the health of our very formidable opponents. We knew in advance that we were in for a hard struggle, and we went on the field determined to play to the best of our ability. I think we did, too; and the reason that we lost is simply that we were up against a team a bit better than ourselves. The margin of victory was only one goal, but I am not going to try to make any excuses or to suggest that we were unlucky to lose. We had our chances as well as our opponents, and the fact is that they made better use of theirs than we did of ours.

It is not my place to single out individual players for special praise, and in any case this would hardly be appropriate. Our opponents' great strength was in their teamwork. Their defence was solid, their attack was swift and co-ordinated, and there was a general harmony in the whole side. That is what we were up against; and although I am sorry we lost, I do not think we disgraced ourselves. For my part I thoroughly enjoyed the match.

Finally, I want to say how much we are looking forward to our next meeting. And I must add that although we admit that the better team won this afternoon, we most certainly do not admit that our opponents will be the better team next time. We have no illusions about the task before us, but we are quite determined that on the occasion of our return match, we shall take the honours.

But that is in the future. For the present, let us do honour where honour is due. Gentlemen, I give you the toast of our opponents, the —— (name of club), coupled with the name of their captain, A—— B——, who, in my opinion, gave one of the finest exhibitions of wing-half play that we have ever seen on this ground.

USEFUL QUOTATIONS

See under Our Opponents (Cricket).

79. REPLY TO THE TOAST OF OUR OPPONENTS (ASSOCIATION FOOTBALL)

Hints.—See under Our Opponents (Cricket).

SPECIMEN

Gentlemen,—On behalf of my team-mates I thank you most heartily for your generous toast. I fear it was too generous. You have made it appear as if the match was one-sided, yet in fact it seemed to me that you had at least as much of the game as we did. Certainly we had a greater share of the luck, and I should not have been surprised if you had claimed that a draw would have been a fairer result.

But the result is of much less importance than the fact that we all had ninety minutes of hard, good, clean soccer. You have been kind enough to praise us for our teamwork. I am not surprised that you should estimate this most highly, for you made it quite clear by your play that you value it above all individual effort. You, sir, made an entirely exaggerated remark about my own performance. Had you been able to see your own play at wing-half, you would have realized that it will need a much better player than I to surpass the reputation you must have earned among your spectators.

Finally, I must thank you for the very hearty reception and magnificent hospitality that you have given us. Shortly you will be coming to visit us. We shall try to return your hospitality as well as we can. If we can beat you again, we

shall do so—but we know that it will be at least as hard a
task as it was this afternoon.

On behalf of the —— (name of club) I thank you.

80. THE TEAMS

Hints.—Sometimes the toast of both teams together is
proposed, and this is especially agreeable when there has
been a big margin of victory. The following specimen can
be used for any team sport.

SPECIMEN

Gentlemen,—It gives me very great pleasure to propose
the toast of the two teams who have entertained us so well
this afternoon. I think everyone who saw the match will
agree that it was a splendid game. Of course one team won,
and the other lost; but I think the winners will forgive me if
I say that, although they deserve our congratulations for their
very fine performance, the result was not the most important
part of the afternoon's entertainment. What pleased me
most—and I think I am speaking for all the spectators—was
the fine spirit in which the game was played. It was hard
fought, yet always in the highest sporting tradition. The
winners never relaxed until the game was over—and the
losers gallantly carried the struggle on right up to the end.

It is not my place to single out individual players on
either side, and in any case I think this would give a false
idea of the match. Both teams played as teams, and the
outstanding feature of the game was the high quality of the
teamwork on both sides. Yet two players, I think, deserve
just a word of special mention. I refer, of course, to the two
captains. Each played a capital game, and each gave his side
fine leadership.

Now, gentlemen, I ask you to drink to the health of the
two teams, —— and —— (names of clubs).

81. SUCCESS TO THE CLUB (CRICKET)

Hints.—This is a common toast at the annual club
dinner, and is generally proposed by the chairman. The

speech should include tributes to the secretary (who will reply to the toast) and other officials, and also to the captain; but unless there has been an exceptionally outstanding player, it is advisable not to single out individual members of the team for special mention, for obvious reasons. However, any success by a club member in representative or other such matches should be mentioned.

SPECIMEN

Gentlemen,—It is my happy duty to rise and remind you of the success the club has enjoyed during the season that has just ended, and to ask you to join me in drinking to continued success in the future.

You do not want me to review our achievements this season. They have already been placed on the record, and we can feel justly proud of them. Our first eleven has won twelve matches, and lost only two; and of the six matches that were drawn, we may fairly say that the weather robbed us of victory at least three times. But I think we have little cause for complaint about the weather this season. It has not been a good summer—English summers rarely are—but a kind Providence has saved most of the rain for week-days and most of the sun for week-ends.

I know you will all support me when I pay tribute to the work of our most energetic secretary and the other officials who have given so freely of their time to make the season the success it has been. It would be invidious if I were to single out any members of the team for special mention, because our victories have been won more by teamwork than anything else, and every man has played his part. But I do not think anyone will object when I remind you of the splendid example set by our captain, A—— B——, who has excelled not only as a fine all-rounder, but also in the sort of leadership that cricket needs. He has been an inspiration to the team. I must also mention the success of one of our younger players, C—— D——, in being chosen to play as an amateur for the County. As you all know, C—— has now signed professional forms with the County, and next season he will be lost to us. Of course we shall miss him seriously; but we shall take pride in his future career, and we wish him all the success he deserves.

Our second eleven has enjoyed less success in actual matches, but its prospects for the future are bright. There has been a welcome influx of youth into the club, and several youngsters have shown in their first season that they will soon be clamouring for places in the first eleven.

You have already seen the report of the club's financial position, and will have observed—no doubt with relief—that we are still solvent. We never want to be much more, but a little extra cash in hand is necessary if we are to keep up our present standard of equipment. As a result of increased costs we have been obliged to raise the subscription for honorary members from —— to ——. No one wants to raise the subscription for playing members; and it is because we are anxious to avoid this that I am taking the liberty of reminding you that the nominal honorary subscription is a minimum sum, and any individual additions to it will be most gratefully received.

Cricket, gentlemen, is an old English game. It is essentially English, and it is by far the oldest of our popular sports. But let us not forget that it was played first—I might almost say invented—by boys. Young lads were wielding home-made bats in the days of Queen Elizabeth, when their elders looked down on the sport as a childish pastime. Now, of course, it is the sport for men of all ages. We ourselves should be hard put if we had to manage without our veterans; but let us remember that cricket is also the game for youth. Ours is quite an old club, but it is young in spirit. As I have said, we have some very promising young players; but we need more, and it is up to us older members to do our best to attract youngsters to join us.

Now, gentlemen, I ask you to join me in drinking to the future success of the club, and with this toast I couple the name of our Honorary Secretary, E—— F——.

USEFUL QUOTATIONS

See under Our Opponents (Cricket).

(Made by the Hon. Secretary)

82. REPLY TO THE TOAST OF SUCCESS TO THE CLUB (CRICKET)
Hints.—This speech usually ends with a toast to the captain of the Club.

SPECIMEN

Mr. Chairman, Gentlemen,—Much as I appreciate the honour you have paid me of coupling my name with this toast, I feel unable to accept your compliments on my own behalf alone. On occasions like this the secretary gets all the credit; but in fact this secretary deserves very little of it. The success and smooth running of the club during the season that has just ended were due to the work of the Committee, of which I am only one member. Teamwork brought the club its success on the field of play; and teamwork also was responsible for the efficient way in which the club has been run off the field.

I must hasten to assure you that I am not trying to shift the blame for my own shortcomings on to the Committee. I do not suggest that it was teamwork that caused the unfortunate misunderstanding at Easter, when we arrived at our opponents' ground at just the same time as they arrived at ours. That was not the fault of the Committee. The blame was all mine—although I can pass a little on to the Postmaster-General, for really the telephone line was bad. On several other occasions the club had to suffer from my sins of omission and commission, and I must tell you that in every case the Committee was quite blameless. For the things that went smoothly they deserve your praise; for the tragedies and disasters, blame me.

I should like to add my personal support to your words, Mr. Chairman, about our captain. A—— B—— is not only a fine player and a fine leader; he is also a fine coach. I have seen him at the nets, putting the youngsters through their paces, and I have seen him giving fielding practice to the team. I have no doubt that the improvement in our standard of match play owes a tremendous amount to the work put in by our captain in coaching and practice.

In thanking you again, therefore, I ask you, gentlemen, to rise again, and drink to the health of our captain, A—— B——. May he have a very long innings.

83. REPLY TO THE TOAST OF THE CLUB CAPTAIN (CRICKET)

SPECIMEN

Mr. Chairman, Gentlemen,—Thank you for your kindness. It should be easy for me to reply to this toast, for I have only to tell you the truth about the way our team has pulled together and the little that has been required of the captain. Unfortunately, with a rather blatant disregard for the truth, my friend the secretary has anticipated my reply, twisted it to suit his own purpose, and modestly sheltered behind it in an attempt to prove that his job was equally simple. I am sure you have not been fooled; and I am sure that the other members of our hard-working Committee will agree with me when I say that the club owes more to its secretary than to any other member.

I am not so modest as the secretary, and I am going to say quite brazenly that in one respect, at least, I think I have carried out my duties as captain extraordinarily well. I must make this boast, because, quite unaccountably, neither you, Mr. Chairman, nor the secretary, has even bothered to mention this most important triumph of mine. As you know, we have played twenty matches during the season; and I, as captain, have won the toss no less than fifteen times! This, I submit, is a proud record. It it the best thing I have done for the club. And I would remind you that I did it all off my own bat. It was a personal achievement that owed nothing to teamwork.

But I am afraid it has been my only personal achievement. Teamwork has done all the rest. I can only say it has been a great honour to me to captain such a team, which deserves our most hearty congratulations. Thank you.

84. SUCCESS TO THE CLUB (ASSOCIATION FOOTBALL)

Hints.—See under Success to the Club (Cricket).

SPECIMEN

Gentlemen,—I believe it was the late Lord Kinnaird, an early President of the F.A., who once celebrated a Cup Final victory by standing on his head in front of the pavilion at the Oval. As he always played in long white flannels and a cricket cap, and had a flowing red beard, it must have been a colourful sight. Sometimes it is said that soccer has lost some of its colour, but that is said of most things. We are constantly being told that we live in a drab world, as if the world was never drab in the past. But can anyone fairly say that soccer today is drab? Whatever it was once, is it not now the most exciting and exhilarating game that was ever invented?

Of course it was not invented really. It just happened, and, like Topsy, just growed. Like nearly every other sport, it was started in England. Now it is played all over the world. British players took it abroad and taught other peoples to play. Now it happens that sometimes the pupils beat the masters, and a great groan goes up about the decline of British soccer. Once upon a time British teams could go across the Channel and rattle up cricket scores against teams that had little idea of the game. Is there any need to regret those days? I don't think so. Nor do I think that British soccer has declined. It is simply that other countries have improved—and the main reason for their improvement has been that British coaches went and taught them the game. Of course we want to win—but even if we do get beaten sometimes, let us rejoice that we have opponents who can now give us a good, hard game.

But my toast is not to the success of soccer in general, or even of British soccer; it is to the success of the club. It is a toast that I can propose with great confidence after the success we have enjoyed during the season that has just ended. You all know our record, and I am sure that you will all join with me in congratulating the team very heartily on its splendid performance. When I say the team I mean the team, and I am not going to mention individuals. At least, I am going to name only one, and I name him not so much for his playing—magnificent as it was—as for his generalship and leadership. Our captain, A—— B——, has inspired the team to play as a team. He has set an example by his own unselfish play, and it is to a great extent due to him that eleven individuals have played the game like one man.

I must say a word also about C—— D——, the captain of our second eleven. It has been his task to encourage and help the younger members of the club, and the results of his work are already beginning to show. Several of the youngsters are now knocking loudly at the first-eleven door, and the fine form shown by the second eleven is the surest sign that the future of the club is going to be at least as good as the past.

Finally, gentlemen, I want to remind you of the great work done by the club officials, and especially the secretary. It was all behind the scenes, but it was worth many goals to us. And that is why, when I ask you to drink this toast, I couple with it the name of E—— F——. Gentlemen— success to the club!

USEFUL QUOTATIONS

See under Our Opponents (Cricket).

85. SUCCESS TO THE CLUB (LAWN TENNIS)

Hints.—See under Success to the Club (Cricket).

SPECIMEN

Ladies and Gentlemen,—In proposing the toast of success to the club. I think I can do no better than express the hope that the club will enjoy as much success next season as it did during the season that has just ended. In only one respect can I hope for something better—and that, of course, is the weather. But I am not going to stress this point too much; because although the weather could be better than it was this year, I need hardly remind you that it has sometimes been a good deal worse.

I think I am voicing the general opinion when I say that we have all had a most enjoyable season. On the courts there was never a dull moment. There were some moments, indeed (here follow with any amusing incident that ocurred during the season).

We have put up a good show in club matches. and our own tournaments have been more successful than ever. I am sure you will all join me in congratulating our new champions, —— —— and —— ——, and in the doubles —— —— and ——. ——, —— —— and —— ——, and —— —— and —— ——.

We are sorry that we are losing two of our oldest members, who are moving to another district. Both —— —— and —— —— have served the club well, and we wish them every success in the game in the future. A happier matter is the admission of several youngsters who, I hope, will shortly be putting their parents in their place.

Whatever doubts I might have about the future of the

club, of one thing I am sure; next season we shall again be delighted by the appearance of our ladies in new fashions which, in mixed doubles, have the effect of making it difficult for the men to keep their eye on the ball. Whenever a new costume appears, I always hear powerful arguments to show that its whole purpose is to enable the wearer to move more freely and play a better game. It would be churlish of me to suggest that this might not be the whole reason, and I am sure I should be doing a disservice to my own sex if I said anything that might deter the ladies from enchanting our eyes as they have done in the past.

Finally, I want to pay my tribute to the club officials, and especially our energetic secretary, who have worked so hard so that we could play.

Ladies and gentlemen, I give you the toast—Success to the club!

USEFUL QUOTATIONS

They also serve who also stand and wait.—*Milton*.

The faith they have in tennis and tall stockings,
Short blistered breeches.   —*Shakespeare*.

See also under Our Opponents (Cricket).

86. THE GOLD MEDALLIST (GOLF)

Hints.—Golf is, of course, one of the most individualist sports, and this speech should be frankly in praise of the winner of the Gold Medal (or whatever other prize has been awarded). Humour is essential, and the speaker should try to include a golf story that has not already been all round the club room.

SPECIMEN

Ladies and Gentlemen,—I am very happy to propose the health of the winner of the Gold Medal, because only a week ago he was my companion in adversity. Actually he was my opponent; but we happened to share the same bunker. I am not going to pretend that our comradeship lasted for long. Mr. —— deserted me with quite unseemly haste, and I was left to continue the excavations by myself. But after the game—and I shan't tell you the result—he expressed his entire agreement with me that the bunker in question—you all know it, I am sure—ought to be removed.

It is a peculiar thing, ladies and gentlemen, that I do not think there is anyone here with whom I have played who has not voiced the same opinion. I won't say you have all kept to that opinion. I will even admit that on occasions —rare ones, I am afraid—I myself have regarded that bunker with a most benevolent eye; but by and large there is a general unanimity of opinion that whoever put that bunker there had a grudge against us. Yet the bunker remains, and I have not yet heard anyone make a formal proposal that it should be removed.

I suppose that every club has its pet hazard of this kind, and for all it has cost us I think you will agree that the course would not be the same without it. I am reminded of a cartoon that appeared in *Punch* many years ago, when the late Benito Mussolini was unchallenged dictator of Italy. The cartoon was inspired by the news that Mussolini was spending a holiday playing golf; and it depicted him with his ball lying badly, and a monstrous bunker in front. Mussolini was standing in his most dictatorial pose, and saying sternly to his caddie: "Remove that bunker!"

The moral, I suppose, is that golf is no game for dictators. It makes you modest. But I do not think Mr. —— needed to take up golf to acquire modesty. He was born modest, and his behaviour after carrying off the Gold Medal has been almost apologetic. He has even been heard to say that it was a fluke. All of you who have seen him play, and those of you who have had the chastening experience of playing against him, will, I know, deny that suggestion indignantly. He was a worthy winner, and he thoroughly deserved his success. Gentlemen—the winner of the Gold Medal!

USEFUL QUOTATIONS

Gentlemen with broad chests and ambitious intentions do sometimes disappoint their friends by failing to carry the world before them.—*Eliot.*

There be some sports are painful, and their labour
   Delight in them sets off.   —*Shakespeare.*

See also under Our Opponents (Cricket).

87. REPLY TO THE TOAST OF THE GOLD MEDALLIST (GOLF)

Hints.—As in the previous speech, a good golfing story that the audience has not heard before is ideal for this.

SPECIMEN

Ladies and Gentlemen,—I feel greatly honoured by your kind reception of this toast. I do not deserve it, any more than I deserve the prize that I happen to have won. There are many golfers here who play a much better game than I do.

If possible, I am even worse at speaking than I am at golf. I have had my attacks of nerves when addressing a ball, but they were nothing compared with my feelings on addressing you now. So I am going to try to hole out in one, and just tell you a little story and then sit down.

(Here insert the golfing story.)

And with that, ladies and gentlemen, I ask you to excuse me. Again, many thanks for your kind toast.

USEFUL QUOTATIONS

See under The Gold Medallist (Golf) *and* Our Opponents (Cricket).

88. SUCCESS TO ANGLING

Hints.—Anglers are proverbially tellers of tall stories, and the speaker should not hesitate to tell a tall one on this occasion. If the speech is to be made at a fairly formal occasion, many ideas will be found in Izaak Walton's *Compleat Angler*.

SPECIMEN

Gentlemen,—After skilfully avoiding the bait for many years, I have at last been hooked. No doubt your chairman, who did the angling, is very pleased with himself. He has landed his victim, and for better or worse the task of proposing this toast is mine. Personally I am sure it could not have been worse; and the chairman is going to find that he made a very poor catch indeed.

The trouble is that I have no idea what to say. I could say that I hope you will all have great success with your angling, and land many large fish; but if I did I shouldn't be telling the truth. Who ever heard of an angler hoping that all the big fish nibbled his rivals' baits? Then, again, I could tell you a tall story—but you wouldn't believe it. So I am going to tell you instead a very simple tale, which you will have no difficulty in swallowing. (Here follow with a very *tall* tale.)

Anglers, gentlemen, have a reputation for jollity. There are pubs scattered all over the country called "The Jolly Angler". You have never seen an inn called "The Gloomy Angler". Yet I doubt if we look very jolly types when we are angling. The explanation, I think, must be that after long periods of enforced silence and patience, we become jolly by way of reaction when we go and slake our thirst. It is fit and proper that we are meeting now in an inn, and I think you have had enough enforced silence and patience while I have been on my feet. So, gentlemen, here's to jollity, and —Success to Angling!

USEFUL QUOTATIONS

Dinna gut your fish till you get them.—*Scottish proverb*.
We may say of Angling as Dr. Boteler said of strawberries: "Doubtless God could have made a better berry, but doubtless God never did"; and so, if I might be a judge, God never did make a more calm, quiet, innocent recreation than angling.—*Izaak Walton*.

89. SUCCESS TO THE ROWING CLUB

Hints.—Most of the hints given already in this chapter will prove useful for this toast.

SPECIMEN

Gentlemen,—Before I ask you to drink to the success of

the club, I must beg you to approve an expression of thanks to two persons. One is our secretary, who not only organized everything with great success throughout the season, but who arranged also this excellent dinner we have just had. The other person to whom we are indebted is the Clerk of the Weather, who gave us some bad breaks at times, but smiled on us in the end.

I am not going to repeat the results of the various events in which we have competed, because you know them already. We have by no means disgraced ourselves, and I am sure that our standard will be at least as high next year.

The object of rowing is, of course, to win the race. But it is the race rather than the victory that counts most, and collecting trophies has its limitations as a pastime. We believe that rowing is a grand sport. I am not trying to underrate the importance of the competitive element, but I do think you will agree when I say that it is the competition itself rather than the result that gives the greatest pleasure.

So, gentlemen, when I ask you to drink to our future success, I should like to think of that word "success" in its broadest sense. Now, gentlemen—raise your glasses, please, and let us drink the toast—Success to the club!

90. REPORT OF THE CLUB SECRETARY

Hints.—This speech may be adapted for any sports club. It is not a toast, but simply a business speech. There is no call for oratory or eloquence. The speech should be factual, and should not include long humorous anecdotes, although a little humour is permissible.

SPECIMEN

Mr. Chairman and Gentlemen,—My report for the season that has just ended will not take long to read. There is no need for me to repeat our match record, for this has already been put up in the clubroom. I know that you will agree that it is a good one.

Our membership now stands at ——. —— members have resigned, owing to leaving the district and for other reasons, and —— new members have been elected. Our future policy with regard to new members will be discussed later in this meeting, so I shall not go into the matter now.

Finance continues to be our biggest headache. You will have seen the statement of accounts prepared by our treasurer, and if you compare this with last season's statement you will see that we have had to pay more for many items and yet have not had any corresponding increase in revenue. I do not want to be alarmist, but I must point out that we shall have to face up to a choice between raising subscriptions or making some economies. That also is a matter that is down for later discussion.

The extension to the pavilion, which was completed at the beginning of the season, has largely solved our previous problem of accommodation for visiting teams, and I do not think any further improvements in this direction will be needed for a time.

We have again arranged a few social events for the winter, and the dates of these will be notified to members within the next few days.

Finally, I should like to remind you of the considerable amount of volunteer work done during the season. Many ladies have given up their time to serve teas, and there was a big response to my early appeal for help on the ground.

In preparation for next season I am going to ask the meeting to authorize me to spend £—— on the following new equipment. (Give details.) Whether we can afford this sum is for the meeting to decide; but I must explain that it is necessary if we are to have the same standard of equipment next season as we have had this year.

That is my report, gentlemen.

USEFUL QUOTATIONS

The English winter—ending in July to recommence in August.—*Lord Byron*.

CHAPTER XII

BUSINESS SPEECHES

91. CHAIRMAN'S SPEECH AT AN ANNUAL GENERAL MEETING

Hints.—This speech will include a brief review of the year's trading, and the Chairman is required only to give the facts. Any attempt at oratory would be out of place, but the Chairman may wish to give his opinion about the future of the Company.

SPECIMEN

Gentlemen,—Before we proceed to the business of this meeting, I have two matters of personal interest to mention. The first is a sad one. I must remind you of the loss we have sustained through the death of Mr. —— ——. As you know Mr. —— was one of our oldest Directors, and he served us well in good times and bad. We shall feel the loss of his wise counsel and shrewd foresight; and still more we shall miss a loyal and sincere friend. On this occasion I should like to record our deep sympathy for his family. (Pause.)

The other personal matter to which I must draw your attention is of a happier kind. It is that Mr. —— ——, who has been a Director for —— years, has been elected a Member of Parliament. I am sure that you will want me, on behalf of the meeting, to congratulate Mr. —— most warmly. Happily the nation's gain will not be our loss; for although Mr. —— will have less time to spend on the Company's affairs, he is remaining on the Board and will continue to give us the benefit of his considerable experience and ability.

Last year's trading, as you will see, was satisfactory from every point of view. Our net profits amounted to £——, which represents an increase of £—— on the previous year. Provision for taxation required £—— (as compared with £—— the previous year). With the amount brought forward there is available for distribution the sum of £——.

A final dividend of 50 per cent, making 65 per cent (less

tax) on Ordinary Share Capital is proposed. This will absorb £——. After appropriations the carry forward is £——.

Our total reserves, including capital reserves, now amount to £——. This represents an increase of £——.

(Now follow with a review of the past year's history relating to buildings, plant, new projects, exports, etc.)

You will see that the volume of our business has risen by over 20 per cent. It is difficult to forecast business conditions in the coming year; but provided that the supply of raw materials is undisturbed, and that prices remain at their present level, there is every reason to believe that our profits will be at least maintained and possibly increased.

During the last year much modernization has been carried out, and in spite of the considerable outlay it is our belief that this has already proved an excellent investment. Further modernization still awaits to be done, and it is our intention to continue this policy as circumstances permit.

Our employees now number ——. Apart from the normal replacements, there have been comparatively few changes of staff during the year. We give a lot of thought to the well-being of our staff, and our Welfare Department has provided (give details). There is a healthy team spirit among the employees of the Company, and I am sure you will wish to join with me in expressing our appreciation of the devotion and loyalty of our staff.

92. PROPOSAL FOR THE ELECTION OF A DIRECTOR OF A COMPANY

(Usually made by the Chairman)

SPECIMEN

Gentlemen,—I have the agreeable task of proposing that a Directorship be awarded to Mr. ——. As you know Mr. —— has served the Company for —— years, and during the last —— years he has held the position of Works Manager. To say that he has carried out his duties efficiently would be an understatement; for he has given the Company not only the benefit of his considerable ability, but a rare devotion and personal enthusiasm for his work. Mr. —— has shown considerable initiative as well as executive powers, and I am convinced that it is in the best interests of the Company that he should now be rewarded with a Directorship.

93. TRADE UNION SECRETARY'S REPORT OF THE YEAR'S WORK

Hints.—A secretary's job is to state the facts clearly and concisely, and no special eloquence is required for this speech. The subject matter will, of course, depend upon the circumstance, and the following specimen may have to be considerably adapted.

SPECIMEN

Mr. Chairman and Gentlemen,—The activities of the Union on behalf of its members during the last year are well known to you, and I do not need to go over them again here. I have, however, a few matters to report. One is that our membership has increased by ——, bringing the total up to ——. This, of course, is the highest number we have ever had in the Union. In the course of the year we held —— meetings, at which the attendances were slightly higher than in the previous year. Our social activities have been increased, and as a result of their popularity it is intended that they should be further expanded next year.

You will have seen the general state of our finances from the copies of the balance sheet that have been circulated. There are one or two items, however, on which you would probably like a few words of explanation. The expenditure on —— was necessitated by ——, etc.

I do not need to make any comment on the matter of——, which was the most important of our activities during the year. As you know, the Union's just claims in this matter were completely met in the end, and our thanks are due to Mr. —— and Mr. ——, who carried out the negotiations for us with great energy and perseverance. The matter of —— is still pending, as you know; and I expect that this will be discussed later during the meeting.

94. SPEECH AT A TRADE UNION MEETING

Hints.—The specimen below is a fairly typical speech that may be adapted for many different sets of circumstances. The speaker should not try to be over-eloquent, but should simply state his points clearly, briefly, and bluntly.

SPECIMEN

Mr. Chairman and Comrades,—There seems to be general agreement among us that we should take vigorous action in the matter of ——, which was sprung on us unexpectedly by the ——. The only question on which we are not agreed is what form this action should take.

My first point is that our action must be swift and vigorous, or else there will be danger of an unofficial strike. Please do not misunderstand me when I call this a danger. I am not using the word in the sense that it is often used in certain sections of the Press. I mean that an unofficial strike would be a danger to us. It would undermine the power of the Union, and that must be avoided at all costs.

My second point is that our action, although swift, should not be hasty. Now I know that the —— has forced this crisis by a hasty and ill-considered action, and that there has been serious provocation. I am not suggesting that we should take it lying down. We have got to stand up for our rights—but let us show more wisdom than they have done. Already the public is generally sympathetic towards us on this matter, in spite of misrepresentation of the issue. If we can keep and increase this public sympathy, we shall win the dispute almost without a fight. The way to do this, I think, is to make a clear and definite statement of our case, and to ensure that it gets the widest publicity. Let us make it plain that we entirely reject the ——'s statement; but in the first instance, at least, let us put our side of the matter in a sensible and reasoned way. If we do this I think we shall win the case, uphold the authority of the Union, and retain public sympathy all at the same time. If we can achieve this, it will be a sure guarantee against any future crisis of this sort.

I therefore propose that we should now (follow with details of proposal, stating points to be made and procedure to be followed).

95. THE PROSPERITY OF THE FIRM

Hints.—This toast, usually proposed at the annual staff dinner or similar function, comes from an employee. A good deal of care must be taken if the speech is to sound both appreciative and sincere. Fulsome flattery of the heads of the firm would be entirely out of place, and would merely cause embarrassment all round. Similarly there should be no suggestion of servility or obsequiousness in the speaker's remarks. But the speech should reflect appreciation and respect in a healthy form.

SPECIMEN

Mr. Chairman, Ladies and Gentlemen,—I can say in all sincerity that I am very pleased to have the honour of proposing the toast of the Firm. This is not merely because I have dined well—although I certainly have; or even because I have wined well—and again, this is no less than the truth. But the thing that makes it so easy and, indeed, pleasurable a task is simply that it is out of office hours. The Firm is, at the moment, a sort of illusion. Seeing all my colleagues here without their ledgers and notebooks, typewriters and telephones, makes me forget the sordid realities of commercial life. Only for the moment, of course. Now if you had asked me to propose the health of the Firm at five-thirty this afternoon, or if you were to ask me to do it at nine-thirty to-morrow morning, I should say—well, never mind what I would say. In any case that's no reflection on the Firm. It's just the matter of my liver.

Now I have been with the Firm for twenty years. I expect to be here another twenty. (I thank you for your reception of that threat.) That will make forty years altogether. Now I ask you, why should I spend nearly the whole of my working life in the service of one Firm? There are only two possible answers. The obvious one, of course, is that I couldn't get another job. The alternative, which I greatly prefer, is that I don't want another job. I like it here.

I'm not going to pretend that I'm one of those rare birds who live for their work. I work for my living. But as working hours make up quite a large proportion of living hours, it seems important that one should be satisfied in one's job. And that satisfaction, very largely, depends on one's Firm. I think this is a good Firm. I like the atmosphere, I like my colleagues, and I like my bosses. I feel that I have a stake in the Firm. So, ladies and gentlemen, I ask you to join me in drinking to its continued prosperity. The Firm!

USEFUL QUOTATIONS

Work, according to my feeling, is as necessary as eating and sleeping.—*Humboldt*.

Many men have been capable of doing a wise thing, many more a cunning thing, but very few a generous thing.—*Pope*.

Corporations have no souls.—*Thurlow*.

Work is the grand cure for all the maladies and miseries that ever beset mankind—honest work.—*Carlyle*.

Man's record upon this wild world is the record of work, and of work alone.—*Holland*.

No man has a right to be idle if he can get work to do, even if he be as rich as Croesus.—*Holland*.

We have a certain work to do for our bread, and that is to be done strenuously; other work for our delight, and that is to be done heartily; neither is to be done by halves or shifts.—*Ruskin*.

In all the world there is nothing so remarkable as a great man, nothing so rare, nothing so well repays study.—*Parker*.

96. REPLY TO THE TOAST OF THE PROSPERITY OF THE FIRM

Hints.—This speech is made by the senior Director present. It should include a refutation of any generous remarks of a personal nature that may have been made by the previous speaker, and an appreciation of the work done by the staff. The importance of teamwork is the keynote. The speaker must take great care to avoid any suggestion of patronage or condescension on the one hand, and yet should not try to force an atmosphere of over-familiarity on the other.

SPECIMEN

Ladies and Gentlemen,—I am very happy to reply to the toast of the prosperity of the Firm, which has been so generously proposed and so cordially received. This fact alone is, I think, the surest guarantee of our future prosperity. For the success of every organization, commercial or otherwise, depends primarily on the co-operation of those who run it, and there is no substitute for good relations and teamwork.

So when I thank you for the toast I must thank you also for all that you have done for the Firm in the last twelve months. I hope you will always think of the Firm not as "it", but as "us"; for it is a simple fact that every one of us here tonight has a real stake in it.

I am not going to talk shop on an occasion like this, but I do want to remind you once again of a matter of internal policy which is very dear to our hearts. Each member of the Firm has his own job to do, and although overlapping is encouraged as far as possible, our business is too complicated to allow us to play musical chairs. But we do want your interest, not only in your own particular job, but in the work of the Firm as a whole; and more than anything else we want your ideas and suggestions for raising our general efficiency even above its present level. I believe that there is nothing so destructive of interest and enthusiasm as a feeling that initiative is not wanted. I assure you that it is here, and that the ideas of the most junior members of the staff are not only always welcomed, but will always be treated with consideration and respect.

That brings me back to teamwork. I think a good Firm should be like a good cricket team—all working together for the common good, and yet not aiming at an equality of performance that can only bring about a standard of mediocrity. We are all, still, individuals with our own particular abilities, and I think that individuality should always be encouraged within the framework of the team.

Finally, I have pleasure in announcing that as from —— our Bonus Scheme will be altered in the following way. (Here give details.) You may be pleased to hear also that the canteen (give details of any project connected with the welfare of the staff).

On behalf of the Firm, ladies and gentlemen, I thank you.

USEFUL QUOTATIONS

See under The Prosperity of the Firm.

97. THE STAFF

Hints.—This toast is proposed by one of the Directors. It should include an expression of the work done by the staff, and emphasis on the importance of teamwork. Broadly speaking, it should follow the same lines as the reply to the toast of the Prosperity of the Firm (No. 96). Again any hint of patronage or condescension must be carefully avoided, but the speaker must not go to the other extreme and try to force over-familiarity.

SPECIMEN

Ladies and Gentlemen,—It is my privilege and pleasure to propose the health of the staff. The reason why it is a pleasure is that I welcome the opportunity to say a few things that I think every day. Whether work is a positive source of enjoyment, or merely a necessary evil, is a matter of opinion—personally I think it is a mixture of both; but there can be no doubt that it is a good deal more pleasant— or, if you like, a good deal less unpleasant—if it is done in a spirit of mutual co-operation. We have that spirit here in a very high degree. I hope we shall always keep it.

Now I am not going to make a high-sounding speech about working for the honour and glory of the Firm. This is a business house, and we are in business to make money; and you work in the Firm with the same primary object. But, as you have shown, there is no reason why even the sordid job of making money should not be made pleasant; and the way to make it pleasant is to work as a team. Teamwork means loyalty, and I know that no staff could be more loyal. I want you to know that your loyalty is appreciated.

I have talked enough. Ladies and gentlemen, I propose the health of the staff, and I couple with this toast the name of our old friend—old in service, but young in spirit— Mr. ——.

USEFUL QUOTATIONS

See under The Prosperity of the Firm.

98. REPLY TO THE TOAST OF THE FIRM

Hints.—*See under* The Prosperity of the Staff.

SPECIMEN

Ladies and Gentlemen,—On behalf of the staff I am happy to reply to this kind toast. It is easy for me to be sincere in my reply, for I have worked here happily for many years. I think my colleagues, old and young, share my happiness; and the fact that we are all so difficult to get rid of explains more than words what we feel about the Firm.

I do not want to get sentimental, because it would be untrue if I were to pretend that the Firm takes up the whole, or even the major part, of our lives. Like many others here tonight, I am a family man, and my greatest joy is in my home. But there is here, too, something of a family spirit —a different sort of family, of course, as it must be; but it exists, and the place would be the poorer without it.

Like everyone else here tonight, I come to work in order to earn my living. But it has always been my simple philosophy that the mere fact that you do something because you have to is no reason for not liking to do it. Ladies and gentlemen, I confess to you that I like my work; or rather, it is not so much my work that I like as the atmosphere in which I do it. I think that everyone contributes to that atmosphere; but it would be most ungenerous of me if I did not say that it could not exist without the active encouragement and participation of the directors. If they have a loyal and co-operative staff, it is what they deserve.

On behalf of the staff I thank you.

USEFUL QUOTATIONS

See under 'The Prosperity of the Firm.

99. PRESENTATION SPEECH ON THE OCCASION OF A RETIRING EMPLOYEE

Hints.—In the specimen it is assumed that the employee is retiring on reaching the age limit. With a very little alteration the speech can be made to serve where an employee is leaving for health reasons or to take another post. The speech must, of course, be generous in praise; but on this sort of occasion the praise tends often to be overdone, with the result that the remarks lose their value.

SPECIMEN

Ladies and Gentlemen,—On an occasion such as this our feelings are bound to be mixed. Mr. Smith is leaving us today.

after thirty years' continuous service with the firm, to enjoy a well-deserved retirement. He takes with him our earnest wishes for his continued health and happiness for many years to come. No one would begrudge Mr. Smith the rest he has earned after his years of hard and selfless work; yet we cannot pretend that we are happy to see him leave us. I do not want to say much about his value to the Firm, because that is a matter of which we shall be reminded, often painfully, for a long time to come. No one is indispensable, but there are some people it is very difficult to do without, as I fear we are shortly going to discover. We are going to miss our Production Manager—but much more are we going to miss Mr. Smith, the man.

As is natural in an organization of this kind, our respective relationships with Mr. Smith have varied a good deal. To some he has been one of the bosses, to be addressed as "Sir". Others have known him just as "Mr. Smith". To others again, he has been simply "Smith"; and to a few intimate colleagues he has been plain "Jack". But his attitude to us has never reflected these differences. He has treated us all with the same unfailing courtesy and good humour. He has never been one to smile at the Directors and scowl at the junior clerks—indeed, from my personal experience he has inclined rather to smiling at the juniors and scowling at the Directors! By his cheerfulness and natural friendliness Mr. Smith has earned the respect of every one of us, and it is with a sense of real loss that we see him go. On behalf of the staff, I have the great pleasure of presenting Mr. Smith with this small token of our esteem and affection. This is a good-bye present, but I hope he will come to see us at times as a friend—if only to look in and gloat. Mr. Smith.

USEFUL QUOTATIONS

See under The Prosperity of the Firm.

100. REPLY TO A FAREWELL PRESENTATION

Hints.—The presentation speech will in some measure govern the reply; but it should be simple, quiet, and, above all, sincere.

SPECIMEN

Ladies and Gentlemen,—There is an Eastern proverb

that says, "In the hum of the market there is money, but under the cherry tree there is rest." Well, I have been in the hum of the market for a good long time. There is a cherry tree in my garden, and it is to my garden that I intend to retire—I did not say rest!

It is difficult for me to realize that today I am leaving this firm where I have worked for so many years. I shall, I think, be quite happy without my work—and, in spite of Mr. Jones's kind words, I have not the slightest doubt that the work will get along very well without me. I was going to say that I have been only a cog in the machine, but I think a happier and more accurate description would be a member of a team. The small part I have played in this team has been made easy for me by the loyal co-operation I have always received from every other member. And it is the thought of leaving this team that makes parting so difficult for me.

Now my innings has come to an end, but I shall watch the future achievements of the team from a seat in the pavilion. You have given me a splendid souvenir to take with me, and I shall always prize this gift and what it stands for. Thank you for your kind present and especially for the kind wishes that have come with it—and good luck to you all!

USEFUL QUOTATIONS

Lost, yesterday, somewhere between sunrise and sunset, two golden hours, each set with sixty diamond minutes. No reward offered, for they are gone for ever.—*Horace Mann*.
See also under The Prosperity of the Firm.

101. PRESENTATION SPEECH TO AN EMPLOYEE GETTING MARRIED

Hints.—A great deal depends on how long the employee has been with the firm. It is assumed in the specimen that he is remaining on the staff; if not (*e.g.*, if the employee is a woman) the specimen should be adapted in conjunction with "Presentation Speech on the Occasion of a Retiring Employee."

SPECIMEN

Ladies and Gentlemen,—I have two pleasant tasks to

perform. One is to offer to Mr. Brown our congratulations and best wishes on the occasion of his marriage; the other is to present him with a small gift from the staff. There is no need for me to say which is the more important of the two jobs. Tomorrow Mr. Brown will go off on his honeymoon, and when we see him again he will be a different man. He will deny it, of course; but he won't deceive any of us.

I have not had the pleasure of meeting the bride, and I can well understand that this pleasure may be long deferred. Not, of course, that Mr. Brown has anything to fear from me; but no doubt he has made out to his wife-to-be that his colleagues are just the sort of persons she would wish him to mix with, and he doesn't want to disappoint her. But I am sure that Mr. Brown has made a splendid choice—he always had good taste; and I know that his bride could not have done better. In such circumstances happiness is a foregone conclusion, and I need only to offer our very best wishes to Mr. and the future Mrs. Brown.

USEFUL QUOTATIONS

See under The Bride and Bridegroom.

102. REPLY TO A PRESENTATION SPEECH ON GETTING MARRIED

Hints.—This speech should be brief and light-hearted.

SPECIMEN

Ladies and Gentlemen,—Thank you very much for your kind gift and good wishes. I am thanking you on behalf of my fiancée as well as myself, and indeed I do look forward to introducing her to you soon. As you may imagine, I have thought quite a bit before taking the plunge, and I really owe a debt to all the married men here. When I first began thinking of getting engaged, I started to look at my married colleagues with new eyes. I watched their expressions when they came to work, and I watched them again when they left. My observations told me that they all seem to thrive on marriage, so I decided to join them. I don't really think you are going to see a new man when I get back from my honeymoon, though—just the old one tamed a bit. Until then, thank you for all you have said, and for this very kind present.

CHAPTER XIII

MISCELLANEOUS TOASTS AND SPEECHES

103. THE PRESS

Hints.—Very often the speaker begins by making a few mildly critical remarks about the Press, just for fun, and then retracts them as his speech continues. This sort of treatment is suitable for an able and experienced speaker, but the novice is advised to play safe and leave out the criticisms.

SPECIMEN

Gentlemen,—From time to time one picks up a newspaper and reads a letter from an irate reader complaining about some item, and solemnly informing the Editor that although he has been a regular reader for the last forty years he will never buy the paper again. I often wonder if these correspondents carry out their threats, or if they get over their annoyance; for on several occasions I have had the same feelings—not with only one paper, but with almost every paper I have read. One reason that I have got over my annoyance in the end is simply the fact that newspapers print such letters. Indeed, the correspondent has only to end up by saying, "Of course you won't dare to print this," to make absolutely sure of seeing his name in print.

This, I think, is typical of one of the outstanding virtues of our newspapers. They are fearless. Of course they give the public what it wants, because a newspaper has got to sell; but they do not shirk from giving unpalatable news and making unpopular comments when these are thought necessary.

Most of our newspapers are to some extent partisan, and it is a fact that if you read the leading articles of two opposing papers on the same day you may get a very different impression of the way the Government is doing its job. But broadly speaking our newspapers keep the opinions to the leaders, and do not mix them up with the simple reporting of the news. The reader can ignore the leaders if he likes. But it is most important that they should appear, and the fact that they differ from one another to such an extent is an excellent sign of the health of the Press as a whole. In some countries you will find that all the newspapers express the same opinions. This makes things much simpler for the readers, of course, but it means that the Press is not free. For it is in the nature of things for different people to hold different views, and the free expression of conflicting views is precisely what we mean by liberty and democracy. When I read two or three conflicting leaders I am sometimes puzzled; but if I ever find that all the leaders are saying the same thing, I shall be seriously alarmed.

It is sometimes said that the Press moulds public opinion. Now I do not think that the representatives of the Press who are with us tonight will take it amiss if I express the view that it would be nearer the truth to say that public opinion moulds the Press. If a citizen has a grievance, if he sees injustice in any department of our social life, his first thought is usually to write to the Press. You all know how many important issues have first come to light as a result of letters of this kind. You all know how many times the responsible authority has had to redress an injustice as a result of the publicity given to it in the Press. But what none of us knows is how many injustices and abuses of office do *not* occur because of the existence of a watchful and fearless Press. I suspect they are numerous, and for this reason above all the freedom of our Press must be held sacred. For the freedom of the Press is the guarantee of our own freedom.

Gentlemen, I ask you to drink to the Press and the health of its representatives who are with us tonight, and I couple with this toast the name of Mr. ——.

USEFUL QUOTATIONS

Four hostile newspapers are to be feared more than a thousand bayonets.—*Napoleon*.

With just enough learning to misquote.—*Lord Byron*.

Amicably if they can, violently if they must.—*De Quincey*.

It is easier to be critical than correct.—*Disraeli*.

Newspapers are the schoolmasters of the common people.
—*Beecher*.

In these times we fight for ideas, and newspapers are our
fortresses.—*Heine*.

Newspapers always excite curiosity. No one ever lays one
down without a feeling of disappointment.—*Charles Lamb*.

104. REPLY TO THE TOAST OF THE PRESS

Gentlemen,—A guilty conscience is a poor thing to have,
especially when you are preparing a speech. I had a guilty
conscience before I came here tonight. I was told that the
health of the Press would be proposed. That meant a speech;
and, knowing the Press as I do, and knowing what its own
representatives say to one another about it when they fore-
gather in odd spots in and about Fleet Street—knowing all
this, I took it for granted that the speech would be at least
partly critical. I was asked to reply, and I prepared a reply
in advance. In it I answered, as well as I could, the sort of
criticisms that I expected to be made.

Now my speech is useless, because instead of criticisms
you have offered only praise. Putting aside my personal dis-
comfiture for the moment, I must say, on behalf of the Press,
that I greatly appreciate the things you have said. Of course
our Press is not perfect by any means, and it will never be
anything but imperfect. But I ask you to believe me when
I say that most of our faults are not malicious. We try to
give the news accurately and without distortion, and when
we fail it is usually because of lack of time, poor communica-
tions, shortage of space, or some other similar cause. As you
know, getting out a newspaper is a hasty business, and haste
is the enemy of accuracy. A philosopher might ask, very
wisely, "Why all the rush?" There is no reason—except that
you, the public, demand it. If any newspaper decided to defer
publication of news for even a few hours, to allow for consideration and double-checking of details, it would soon
lose its customers.

I was pleased that the proposer of this toast made the
point that public opinion has more influence on the Press
than the Press has on public opinion. It is a common criticism
of newspapers that for privately owned concerns they have

too much power to make people think along certain lines. This criticism does not flatter the public, and I think it is entirely false. The function of the Press is to allow for the free expression of public opinion, not to try to dictate it. The very fact that newspapers are competitive makes them sensitive to public opinion, for it is on the public's opinion of a newspaper that its circulation depends.

This does not mean that we are unconscious of our responsibilities. We know that the Press has power; we think it is good that it should have power, so long as it is used to express the views and wishes of the community as a whole; and we shall continue to try to do our duty to the community to the best of our ability.

Gentlemen, on behalf of the Press I thank you.

(After the applause, follow with "Auld Lang Syne".)

105. VOTE OF THANKS TO A LECTURER

Hints.—It is difficult to give general advice on this speech, for its contents and style will depend very largely on the subject of the lecture that has been given. For example, a vote of thanks to a Professor of Archæology who has lectured on Roman Britain would be entirely different from a vote of thanks to a professional cricketer who has given a talk on spin bowling. The following specimen, which is a vote of thanks to a temperance lecturer, must therefore be regarded as typical only to a limited extent.

SPECIMEN

Ladies and Gentlemen,—I am sure I am speaking on behalf of the whole audience when I say that Mr. —— has given us a remarkably instructive, lucid, and interesting talk. In my experience lectures on this subject all too often rely on sentimental and emotional appeals. Mr. —— has certainly not neglected the human aspect of his theme, and indeed he has drawn a vivid and graphic picture of the social and moral effects of alcoholism; but he has placed his case on hard facts, and he has marshalled these in a way that to me, at any rate, makes them completely irrefutable. His arguments were entirely free from bigotry and narrow-minded prejudice, and the evidence he has brought forward is as conclusive as it is startling. I am convinced that no one can leave this hall without having been deeply affected by this lecture—for it is talks of this kind that can do more than anything else to combat the evils of drink. It remains for me only to propose a very hearty vote of thanks to Mr. —— for his admirable lecture.

USEFUL QUOTATIONS

Alcohol—liquid madness sold at 10d. the quartern.—*Carlyle*.

If abstinence on the part of a temperate drinker would reclaim any drunkard, a man of ordinary humanity would practise it as far as considerations of enjoyment were concerned.—*Lord Bramwell*.

O thou invisible spirit of wine! if thou hast no name to be known by, let us call thee devil.—*Shakespeare*.

106. VOTE OF THANKS TO AN AMATEUR DRAMATIC SOCIETY

Hints.—This speech is usually made after a performance by the Society. It should be brief, and the speaker should be careful not to single out individual actors and actresses. The speech should always include a generous tribute to the work of the people behind the scenes.

SPECIMEN

Ladies and Gentlemen,—On behalf of the audience I should like to thank you all for the wonderful show you have given us. We expected it to be good, for we know how enthusiastic you have been in preparing for it; but I am sure that none of us expected the production to be of this high standard. I only wish that some of the London critics had come here and seen what can be done by amateurs who combine enthusiasm and ability in such a high degree.

I am not going to praise any of the cast singly, because if I did that I should in honesty be bound to praise every one of you. You all played your parts superbly. But I hope you will forgive me if I do single out a few members of your Society for special mention. They are not on the stage, and indeed we have not seen them; but we have seen the results of their work behind the scenes, and it would be impossible to praise this too highly.

When I add that I wish the Society every success in the future I am merely saying that I hope you will soon have another show ready for our delight. Again, on behalf of the audience, thank you very much.

107. OUR AUSTRALIAN GUESTS

Hints.—This speech can be adapted for use in proposing the toast to visitors from any of the other Dominions. It should stress the links that bind the countries of the Commonwealth, and the greatest care should be taken to avoid any suggestion of patronage.

SPECIMEN

Ladies and Gentlemen,—The days of Imperial jingoism are over, and I do not think any of us regret their passing. The old conception of the British Empire has given way to the much finer ideal of the British Commonwealth of Nations. The ties that now bind us together are less obvious but far stronger than before, because they rest on sounder foundations. We have much to be proud of in the achievements of the old Empire; but our greatest pride must surely lie in the way it has developed into the Commonwealth as it is today. It is an example to the world of how free, democratic peoples, separated from one another by many thousands of miles, can live together in a voluntary association based on goodwill and mutual help. The solidarity of that association has twice been sorely tested during this century, and on each occasion it has gained from the ordeal. At the beginning of the Second World War, I remember, we from the Old Country used to call ourselves "British troops", and we were at first puzzled when an official directive assigned us the description of "United Kingdom troops". In our thoughtless vanity it had not occurred to us that other people of the Commonwealth also took a pride in being called British!

The achievements of Australia's fighting men need no fresh recital from me now. They are too well known, and have taken an honoured place in history. Little good comes out of the evils of war; but those of us who were privileged to serve alongside Australian troops gained a new experience in comradeship that will never be forgotten. I do not need to remind you how that spirit has continued in the happier days of peace. When this country entered the long struggle for recovery, it was the Australians who were the first to give us the help we so badly needed. It was the Australians who sent us food—not out of any surplus of their own, but by pure self-denial. When our food was severely rationed through force of necessity, the Australians rationed themselves simply in order to help us. We shall never forget this.

The British are often accused of paying too much attention to sport. We in the Old Country acknowledge the fault, and I think I am right in saying that the Australians also plead guilty to the charge. If the Test Matches mean as much to them as they do to us, then they are very important events indeed. Their true significance goes far beyond the scoreboard. To both of us sport means not only playing a game, but sportsmanship and fair play. The Australians excel at many sports besides cricket; but what arouses our admiration most is their supreme excellence in the quality of sportsmanship. Ladies and gentlemen, I give you the toast of our Australian guests.

108. OUR AMERICAN GUESTS

Hints.—Stress should be placed on the common language and the partnership in efforts to preserve world freedom.

SPECIMEN

Ladies and Gentlemen,—Is is my privilege to propose the toast of our American guests. According to the Home Office, I believe, they come under the category of aliens. I have never met people less alien in my life. They belong to the same English-speaking family as ourselves, and I hope they will consider themselves at home as long as they are in this country.

In fact I do not really need to express this hope, for the Americans, themselves so wonderfully hospitable, are quick to settle down. You remember the G.I.s during the war. You remember how they invaded our pubs, drank our beer, and then, when they went home again, took our girls with them! Why, I even saw some G.I.s at Lords!

The other day I met an American in the street. It was Baker Street actually, and this gentleman was wearing a brightly coloured tie, a complicated-looking camera, and a puzzled frown. "Excuse me," he said, "but can you tell me where Sherlock Holmes used to live? I just can't find the number."

I told him, as gently as I could, that Sherlock Holmes had never lived at all. At first he thought I was pulling his leg; but when he realized that this was the cold truth, I could see that he was disappointed and even hurt. "Well," he said, "I guess that's too bad. It was one of the things I was looking forward to see." At that moment I felt deeply sorry that Sherlock Holmes had not lived in Baker Street. For Sherlock Holmes, while certainly not typical, was very English; and it was for that reason, I think, that this American was so interested in him.

The Americans are proud of their way of life, and rightly so. We, too, are proud of ours. Often we compare the two, sometimes to the advantage of one and sometimes to the advantage of the other. Yet, although there are many differences, there are more points of similarity; and on fundamentals—the ideas of decency and freedom and justice—the two peoples are entirely at one.

America and Britain have fought together in two world wars. The two countries have fought under a unified command, and shared both setbacks and victory. At the end of the Second World War, Britain was hard hit economically. America generously came to our aid. Since then the world has gone through a trying time, and the price of peace has been eternal vigilance. In keeping that peace our two countries have worked together harmoniously, with the same kind of co-operation that characterized our joint Forces during the war. I am convinced that our friendship with the great United States of America is one of the strongest bulwarks of peace in the world today.

Ladies and gentlemen, I give you the toast of our guests from the United States.

109. OUR FRENCH GUESTS

Hints.—The speaker should stress the alliance with France and the close cultural and economic bonds.

SPECIMEN

Ladies and Gentlemen,—It is with very great pleasure that I rise to greet our guests from France. A great French writer once said, "Everyone has two countries: his own, and France." I should be tempted to say that the French are unlucky in having only one; but there is no need to be sorry for them—for that one country is France.

France is our closest neighbour, and I do not mean merely geographically. The ties that bind our two countries are very strong in every field of human life. And we must acknowledge that the French have done much to prevent us from being more insular than we already are. Every year thousands of Britains cross that strip of water that we rather arrogantly call the English Channel, and spend a holiday in a country that seems to them to be one huge holiday resort. They come back with happy memories, and so our common link is strengthened over and over again.

Many years ago we used to fight the French. Eventually both of us came to our senses, and for a long time now any conflict between our two peoples has been unthinkable. What is more, there can never again be any question of either country remaining neutral in the event of the other being committed to fight in a major war. We are permanent allies, in peace as well as in war. In the two World Wars France has suffered grievously, experiencing the horrors of occupation by an aggressor. But even while occupied, France fought on; and one of the most glorious chapters in her history was written by the heroes of the French Resistance.

Now both countries are free again, and the preservation of their joint freedom depends to a great extent on their mutual co-operation. It is a good omen that the Entente Cordiale has never been more cordial than it is today.

Ladies and gentlemen,—I give you the toast of our guests from France!

110. IN AID OF CHARITY

Hints.—This speech will obviously depend to a great

extent on the particular charity involved; but the specimen has been made on general lines, so that most of it will be of use for almost any occasion of this kind.

SPECIMEN

Ladies and Gentlemen,—There is an unfortunate danger today in the idea that charity appeals are out of date and unnecessary. We have a Welfare State. In theory, we are all provided for from the cradle to the grave. The hospitals, and indeed the whole health service, are financed by compulsory insurance and taxation. Unemployment relief, public assistance, and pensions are similarly provided. It is easy— fatally easy—to conclude from this that charity is no longer necessary.

Of course charity is no longer so necessary as it was. Of course there are fewer charities in the country. No one is going to regret this. But there still are charities, because there still are good causes that do not come within the framework of the national welfare scheme. The charity that I am asking you to support today is one of these. I do not think anyone will doubt that it is a good cause; and it is a definite fact that it cannot continue to exist without private assistance.

In theory it should be easier to obtain this assistance now that there are fewer charities; but in fact the reverse is the case. Partly this is because people are too ready to think that charities are no longer necessary, and partly because the State schemes have to be financed by all of us, including those who formerly gave voluntarily to charities. The subscriptions that we receive today are less than they were, and our costs have greatly increased. You know that nothing is wasted on administrative expenses—indeed, a very large part of the work is done voluntarily. Those who do this work are making their contribution, and a very valuable one it is. I ask you to make yours. However small it is, it will be a great help; and I do not think you will ever regret having given it.

CHAPTER XIV

FURTHER USEFUL QUOTATIONS

Blessed is the man who, having nothing to say, abstains from giving us wordy evidence of the fact.—*George Eliot*.

In general those who have nothing to say contrive to spend the longest time in doing it.—*J. R. Lovell*.

I am no orator, as Brutus is;
But, as you know me all, a plain blunt man.
                    —*Shakespeare, "Julius Caesar"*.

I would be loath to cast away my speech, for beside that it is excellently well penn'd, I have taken great pains to con it.—*Shakespeare, "Twelfth Night"*.

Do you want people to speak well of you? Then do not speak at all yourself.—*Pascal*.

As a vessel is known by the sound, whether it be cracked or not; so men are proved, by their speeches, whether they be wise or foolish.—*Demosthenes*.

Be sure to leave other men their turns to speak.—*Francis Bacon*.

Let him now speak, or else hereafter for ever hold his peace.—*Book of Common Prayer (Solemnization of Matrimony)*.

I don't care where the water goes if it doesn't get into the wine.—*G. K. Chesterton*.

Many, being reasonable, must get drunk;
The best of life is but intoxication.—*Lord Byron*.

"It wasn't the wine," murmured Mr. Snodgrass in a broken voice, "it was the salmon."—*Charles Dickens, "Pickwick Papers"*.

No speech ever uttered or utterable is worth comparison with silence.—*Thomas Carlyle*.

He had only one vanity: he thought he could give advice better than any other person.—*Mark Twain*.

No fools are so troublesome as those who have some wit. —*La Rochefoucauld.*

It is true we are creatures of circumstance, but circumstances are also, in a great measure, the creatures of us.— *Lord Lytton.*

Remember what Simonides said—that he never repented that he had held his tongue, but often that he had spoken. —*Plutarch.*

It is a sad thing when men have neither wit to speak well nor judgment to hold their tongues.—*La Bruyère.*

Intemperance in talk makes a dreadful havoc in the heart. —*Wilson.*

The true use of speech is not so much to express our wants as to conceal them.—*Oliver Goldsmith.*